Debunking The Myth of Non-Binary Gender, and The Problem With Gender Identity

By

Julian Henley

Copyright (c) Julian Henley 2023

Other works by Julian Henley:

"The Anatomy of a Healthy Marriage"

"Dickie A Cumming: The Prequel (Part I)" - anti-woke visual novel available to download at Steam Games

Part 1: The Problem With Gender Identity

Chapter 1: The Perilous Path of Identity Politics: Unveiling the Threat to Society

Introduction

In recent years, a dangerous ideology has been gaining traction in society, threatening to tear apart the very fabric of our communities. This ideology, known as identity politics, has infiltrated various aspects of our lives, from politics and education to social interactions and even entertainment. While on the surface it may appear to promote inclusivity and equality, a closer examination reveals a perilous path that leads to division, intolerance, and the erosion of individual freedoms.

This chapter aims to introduce the dangers and problems associated with identity politics. By exploring its origins, examining its impact on society, and highlighting the risks it poses to our collective well-being, I hope to raise awareness about this alarming trend and encourage critical thinking about its implications.

The Origins of Identity Politics

Identity politics emerged as a response to historical injustices and systemic inequalities faced by marginalized groups. It sought to give voice to those who had long been silenced and ignored. However, what began as a noble pursuit for justice has morphed into something far more insidious.

The roots of identity politics can be traced back to postmodernist theories that gained popularity in academic circles during the latter half of the 20th century. Postmodernism rejected universal truths and objective reality in favor of subjective experiences and multiple interpretations of truth. This rejection of objective reality laid the groundwork for the rise of identity politics.

By emphasizing individual identities based on race, gender, sexuality, and other characteristics, identity politics seeks to divide people into distinct groups with competing interests. It encourages individuals to view themselves primarily through the lens of their identity, rather than as unique individuals with a multitude of experiences and perspectives.

The Impact on Society

Identity politics has permeated every aspect of our society, from politics and education to media and entertainment. Its influence can be seen in the rise of identity-based movements, such as Black Lives Matter and #MeToo, which have brought attention to important issues but have also fostered a divisive mentality.

One of the most concerning aspects of identity politics is its tendency to stifle free speech and open dialogue. In an environment where certain viewpoints are deemed unacceptable or offensive based on the identity of the speaker, honest conversations become nearly impossible. This leads to the prevention of intellectual discourse and hampers our ability to address complex societal issues.

Furthermore, identity politics promotes a suffering mentality, where individuals are encouraged to see themselves as perpetual victims of oppression. This victimhood narrative not only undermines personal agency and resilience but also perpetuates a cycle of blame and resentment.

The Risks and Dangers

Identity politics poses significant risks to our society. By prioritizing group identities over individuality, it fosters division and animosity among different communities. It encourages tribalism, where people are more likely to associate with those who share their identity markers rather than engaging with diverse perspectives.

Moreover, identity politics undermines the principles of meritocracy and equal opportunity. Instead of focusing on individual achievements and qualifications, it promotes the idea that certain groups deserve preferential treatment based solely on their identity. This not only perpetuates discrimination but also hinders social progress by devaluing individual accomplishments.

Another danger of identity politics is its potential to erode the very foundations of our democratic society. By prioritizing group rights and interests over individual rights and freedoms, it threatens the principles of equality and justice that our society is built upon. It creates a hierarchy of persecution complex, where certain groups are deemed more deserving of protection and support than others.

Conclusion

Identity politics, once a well-intentioned response to historical injustices, has evolved into a dangerous ideology that threatens the cohesion and progress of our society. By dividing people into competing groups based on their identities, it fosters division, stifles free speech, and undermines individual freedoms.

It is crucial that we recognize the risks and dangers associated with identity politics and engage in open dialogue about its implications. Only through critical thinking and a commitment to individuality can we navigate the perilous path of identity politics and strive for a more inclusive and harmonious society.

In the following chapters, I aim to explore many of these concepts in more detail.

Chapter 2: The Illusion of Unity: How Identity Politics Divides Us

In today's society, identity politics has become a pervasive force, infiltrating every aspect of our lives. It promises to champion diversity and inclusivity, but beneath its seemingly noble facade lies a dangerous ideology that can be damaging. This chapter aims to expose the illusion of unity created by identity politics and shed light on the divisive consequences it brings.

The Dangerous Consequences

Identity politics has led to the creation of echo chambers, where individuals only engage with those who share their identities and beliefs. This tribalistic mentality stifles open dialogue and critical thinking, as dissenting opinions are seen as an attack on one's identity rather than an opportunity for growth.

Furthermore, identity politics perpetuates a downtrodden mentality that hinders progress. By constantly emphasizing the ways in which individuals have been oppressed, it discourages personal responsibility and agency. Instead of empowering individuals to overcome obstacles, it encourages them to view themselves as perpetual victims.

Moreover, identity politics fosters division among different marginalized groups. It creates a hierarchy of oppression, where certain identities are deemed more valuable or deserving of attention than others. This not only undermines the solidarity that should exist among marginalized communities but also perpetuates a cycle of competition and resentment.

The Illusion of Unity

Identity politics claims to promote unity by celebrating diversity, but in reality, it only reinforces divisions. By fixating on our differences rather than our shared humanity, it erodes the very foundations of a cohesive society.

True unity can only be achieved through a recognition of our commonalities and a commitment to shared values. Identity politics, however, encourages us to view each other as adversaries rather than allies. It fosters an partisan mindset that hinders progress and perpetuates animosity.

Moving Beyond Identity Politics

To overcome the dangers of identity politics, we must shift our focus from divisive identity markers to the universal principles that bind us together. We must recognize that true progress can only be achieved through collaboration and understanding.

This does not mean ignoring or erasing the unique experiences and struggles faced by different groups. Rather, it means acknowledging these differences while also recognizing our shared humanity. It means fostering empathy and compassion for all individuals, regardless of their identities.

By moving beyond identity politics, we can create a society that celebrates diversity without sacrificing unity. We can build bridges instead of walls and work towards a future where everyone is valued for their individual merits rather than their group affiliations.

Conclusion

Identity politics may have started with good intentions, but it has devolved into a divisive ideology that threatens to tear us apart. Its emphasis on individual identities over shared humanity undermines the very fabric of our society.

We must reject the illusion of unity created by identity politics and instead strive for a society that values diversity while fostering a sense of common purpose. Only then can we truly overcome the divisions that plague us and work towards a more inclusive and united future.

Chapter 3: The Tyranny of Labels: How Identity Politics Reduces Individuals to Stereotypes

From politics to academia, from social media to corporate boardrooms, the tyranny of labels has taken hold, reducing individuals to nothing more than stereotypes.

The Danger of Reductionism

Identity politics reduces individuals to nothing more than stereotypes. It ignores the complexity and diversity within groups and instead lumps people together based on superficial characteristics. This reductionism is not only intellectually lazy but also deeply dehumanizing.

When we reduce individuals to labels such as black, white, male, or female, we strip them of their unique experiences, talents, and perspectives. We deny them the opportunity to be seen as individuals with agency and autonomy. Instead, they become mere representatives of their group, forced to conform to the expectations and narratives imposed upon them.

Furthermore, this reductionism perpetuates a divisive us group bias. It fosters an environment where individuals are pitted against each other based on their group identities. Instead of fostering understanding and empathy, identity politics breeds resentment and animosity.

The Illusion of Progress

Identity politics promises progress and social justice, but in reality, it perpetuates a cycle of perceived persecution and dependency. By framing individuals as victims of systemic oppression, it absolves them of personal responsibility and agency.

This victim mentality undermines the principles of individualism and self-determination that are essential for personal growth and success. It fosters a culture of entitlement and entitlement leads to stagnation.

Furthermore, identity politics creates a hierarchy of victimhood where certain groups are deemed more oppressed than others. This leads to a never-ending competition for victim status, where individuals vie for recognition and validation based on their perceived level of suffering.

Moving Beyond Identity Politics

It is time to reject the tyranny of labels and move beyond the limitations of identity politics. We must recognize that individuals are more than the sum of their group identities. We must celebrate our shared humanity and embrace the diversity and complexity within each individual.

Instead of focusing on what divides us, we should strive to find common ground and build bridges of understanding. We should encourage open dialogue and intellectual diversity, allowing for the free exchange of ideas and perspectives.

By rejecting identity politics, we can reclaim our individuality and freedom. We can create a society that values individuals for who they are, not what group they belong to. It is only through this rejection that we can truly achieve a just and equitable society.

Chapter 4: The Erosion of Free Speech: Identity Politics and the Suppression of Dissent

Under the guise of promoting equality and inclusivity, identity politics has created a climate of fear and intolerance, where any dissenting opinion is met with hostility and censorship. This erosion of free speech is not only detrimental to our democratic values but also hinders intellectual progress and stifles the exchange of ideas.

Under the banner of identity politics, any criticism or disagreement is labeled as hate speech or bigotry. This tactic effectively shuts down any meaningful dialogue and prevents the exploration of alternative perspectives. Dissenters are branded as oppressors or enablers of oppression, effectively silencing their voices and undermining their credibility.

The Suppression of Dissent

One of the most alarming consequences of identity politics is the suppression of dissenting opinions. In an environment where certain ideas are deemed unacceptable or offensive, individuals are discouraged from expressing their thoughts openly for fear of retribution. This self-censorship not only stifles intellectual growth but also creates an belief reinforcement zones where only one perspective is allowed to prevail.

Universities, once bastions of free thought and open debate, have become breeding grounds for this culture of suppression. Speakers with controversial views are disinvited or shouted down, denying students the opportunity to engage with diverse ideas and challenge their own beliefs. This intellectual homogeneity not only limits the educational experience but also hinders the development of critical thinking skills.

Furthermore, social media platforms have become battlegrounds for ideological warfare, where dissenting voices are often targeted and harassed. The fear of online backlash and public shaming has led many individuals to self-censor their opinions, effectively eroding the marketplace of ideas that is essential for a healthy democracy.

The Importance of Free Speech

Free speech is a fundamental right that is essential for the functioning of a democratic society. It enables individuals to express their opinions, beliefs, and ideas without fear of censorship or persecution. Free speech is crucial for the exchange of ideas, the challenging of existing norms, and the pursuit of truth. It allows for the expression of dissenting voices and alternative perspectives, which are essential for progress and innovation. Without free speech, progress becomes stagnant, as dissenting voices are silenced and alternative perspectives are ignored. The suppression of free speech can lead to a lack of diversity in thought and a narrowing of perspectives. This can result in a society that is closed-minded and resistant to change. It is important to defend free speech against the encroachment of identity politics. Identity politics can lead to the suppression of free speech by creating an environment where certain ideas are deemed unacceptable or offensive. This can lead to self-censorship and a reluctance to express certain opinions or ideas. To ensure that free speech is protected, it is necessary to create spaces where all ideas can be openly debated and challenged without fear of reprisal. This requires fostering an environment that values intellectual diversity and encourages respectful dialogue. It is important to promote critical thinking and encourage individuals to challenge their own beliefs and assumptions. In conclusion, free speech is essential for the functioning of a democratic society. It allows for the exchange of ideas, the challenging of existing norms, and the pursuit of truth. To ensure that free speech is protected, it is necessary to create an environment that values intellectual diversity and encourages respectful dialogue. We must defend free speech against the encroachment of identity politics and promote critical thinking to ensure that all voices are heard.

Conclusion

Identity politics poses a significant threat to free speech and open discourse. By suppressing dissent, promoting groupthink, and creating an atmosphere of fear and intolerance, this ideology undermines the very foundations of our democratic society. It is imperative that we recognize the dangers of identity politics and actively work towards reclaiming the principles of free speech and intellectual freedom.

Chapter 5: The Weaponization of Victimhood: How Identity Politics Exploits Suffering for Political Gain

In recent years, identity politics has become a powerful force in shaping public discourse and political movements. While the initial goal of identity politics was to give voice to marginalized groups and address historical injustices, it has since evolved into a dangerous ideology that weaponizes victimhood for political gain. This chapter explores how identity politics exploits suffering, perpetuates division, and undermines the pursuit of true equality.

The Rise of Victimhood Culture

Identity politics thrives on the cultivation of victimhood culture, where individuals are encouraged to see themselves primarily as victims of systemic oppression. This culture promotes the idea that one's identity group determines their worth and moral authority, creating a hierarchy of victimhood. The more victimized an individual or group claims to be, the greater their perceived moral authority becomes.

This hierarchy of victimhood not only fosters a sense of entitlement among certain groups but also stifles open dialogue and debate. Any dissenting opinion is immediately dismissed as an attack on the oppressed, effectively silencing opposing viewpoints and hindering intellectual growth.

The Weaponization of Suffering

Identity politics weaponizes suffering by using it as a tool to gain power and control. By framing every issue through the lens of oppression, proponents of identity politics can manipulate public sentiment and advance their own agenda.

For example, when discussing policy issues such as immigration or criminal justice reform, identity politics often focuses solely on the experiences of marginalized groups without considering the broader implications for society as a whole. This narrow focus not only ignores the complexities of these issues but also undermines efforts to find practical solutions that benefit everyone.

Furthermore, identity politics encourages individuals to view themselves as perpetual victims, fostering a culture of grievance and resentment. This victim mentality not only hinders personal growth and resilience but also perpetuates a cycle of blame and division.

The Divisive Nature of Identity Politics

Identity politics thrives on division, pitting different identity groups against each other in a never-ending battle for recognition and power. By emphasizing differences rather than commonalities, identity politics undermines the pursuit of true equality.

Instead of fostering unity and understanding, identity politics fosters tribalism and animosity. It encourages individuals to view those outside their own identity group as enemies, perpetuating a group biased mentality that hinders social progress.

Moreover, identity politics often reduces complex issues to simplistic narratives of oppressor versus oppressed. This oversimplification not only fails to address the underlying causes of inequality but also alienates potential allies who may be sympathetic to the cause but do not fit neatly into the prescribed categories.

The Erosion of Individuality

One of the most insidious effects of identity politics is the erosion of individuality. By reducing individuals to mere representatives of their identity group, identity politics denies the complexity and diversity within each person.

This reductionist approach not only undermines personal autonomy but also stifles intellectual growth and creativity. It discourages individuals from thinking for themselves and instead encourages conformity to the dominant narrative of victimhood.

Furthermore, identity politics promotes a culture of self-censorship, where indiv duals are afraid to express dissenting opinions for fear of being labeled as oppressive or insensitive. This stifling of free expression undermines the principles of open dialogue and intellectual diversity that are essential for a healthy democracy.

Moving Beyond Identity Politics

To truly address the issues of inequality and injustice, we must move beyond the limitations of identity politics. We must recognize that individuals are more than just their identity group and that true equality can only be achieved through a focus on shared humanity.

This requires fostering a culture of empathy and understanding, where individuals are encouraged to listen to and learn from each other's experiences without reducing them to simplistic narratives of victimhood. It also requires a commitment to finding common ground and working towards practical solutions that benefit everyone, rather than perpetuating division and grievance.

Conclusion

In conclusion, identity politics has become a dangerous ideology that exploits suffering for political gain. By weaponizing victimhood, perpetuating division, and eroding individuality, identity politics undermines the pursuit of true equality. It is time to move beyond the limitations of identity politics and embrace a more inclusive and empathetic approach to social change.

Chapter 6: The Danger of Groupthink: Identity Politics and the Death of Critical Thinking

Identity politics now operates on the premise that an individual's identity is the most important aspect of their being. It reduces complex individuals to a single dimension, defining them solely by their race, gender, sexual orientation, or other immutable characteristics. This reductionism not only oversimplifies the human experience but also creates an environment ripe for groupthink.

The Dangers of Groupthink

Groupthink occurs when individuals prioritize consensus and conformity over critical thinking and independent thought. In an environment dominated by identity politics, dissenting opinions are often dismissed as invalid or even harmful. This stifling of intellectual diversity undermines the very foundations of a healthy democracy.

When individuals are encouraged to view themselves primarily as members of a particular group, they are more likely to adopt a herd mentality. They conform to the prevailing beliefs and values within their group without questioning or critically examining them. This conformity leads to a dangerous homogenization of thought, where alternative perspectives are silenced and marginalized.

Furthermore, groupthink discourages individuals from engaging in rigorous debate and intellectual discourse. Instead of engaging with opposing viewpoints, individuals retreat into insular thinking squeres where their beliefs are reinforced and dissenting voices are ignored. This echo chamber effect perpetuates a cycle of confirmation bias, where individuals only seek out information that aligns with their pre-existing beliefs.

The Death of Critical Thinking

Critical thinking is the cornerstone of a well-functioning society. It allows us to question assumptions, challenge prevailing narratives, and arrive at informed conclusions. However, identity politics undermines critical thinking by discouraging individuals from questioning the prevailing orthodoxy.

In an environment dominated by identity politics, any criticism or questioning of the prevailing narrative is often labeled as oppressive or bigoted. This creates a chilling effect on free speech and intellectual inquiry. Individuals fear speaking out for fear of being ostracized or labeled as enemies of progress.

Moreover, identity politics promotes a victimhood mentality that discourages personal responsibility and agency. It fosters a culture of blame and entitlement, where individuals are encouraged to see themselves as perpetual victims rather than empowered agents of change. This victimhood mentality stifles personal growth and hinders the development of resilience and self-reliance.

The Path Forward

To reclaim critical thinking and intellectual diversity, we must challenge the dominance of identity politics in our society. We must encourage open dialogue, respectful debate, and the free exchange of ideas. We must create spaces where individuals feel safe to express dissenting opinions without fear of retribution.

Furthermore, we must recognize that individuals are more than the sum of their identities. We must reject reductionism and embrace the complexity and nuance of the human experience. By doing so, we can foster a society that values individuality, intellectual curiosity, and the pursuit of truth.

In conclusion, identity politics poses a grave threat to critical thinking and intellectual diversity. Its unchecked growth has led to a dangerous erosion of individuality and a stifling of dissenting voices. To preserve the foundations of a healthy democracy, we must challenge the dominance of identity politics and reclaim the importance of critical thinking in our society.

Chapter 7: The Paradox of Intersectionality: How Identity Politics Creates Hierarchies of Oppression

Introduction

The very ideology that claims to fight against oppression and hierarchies ends up creating its own hierarchies of oppression. This chapter explores the paradox of intersectionality, the cornerstone of identity politics, and how it perpetuates divisions and fosters a culture of victimhood.

The Origins of Intersectionality

Intersectionality emerged as a concept in the late 1980s, coined by legal scholar Kimberlé Crenshaw. It aimed to address the unique experiences and challenges faced by individuals who belong to multiple marginalized groups. Intersectionality recognizes that people's identities are complex and interconnected, shaped by factors such as race, gender, sexuality, class, and disability.

The Paradox Unveiled

While intersectionality initially sought to promote inclusivity and understanding, it has morphed into a divisive ideology that perpetuates hierarchies of oppression. By emphasizing differences rather than commonalities, identity politics inadvertently creates a system where certain identities are deemed more oppressed than others.

The Hierarchy of Victimhood

One of the most troubling consequences of intersectionality is the creation of a hierarchy of victimhood. According to this hierarchy, individuals with multiple marginalized identities are seen as more oppressed and therefore more deserving of attention and resources. This leads to a dangerous competition for victimhood status, where individuals vie for recognition as the most oppressed.

The Silencing of Dissenting Voices

Identity politics also stifles dissenting voices and discourages open dialogue. Those who challenge the prevailing narrative are often labeled as privileged or oppressive, regardless of the validity of their arguments. This silencing of dissent undermines the principles of free speech and intellectual diversity, essential for a healthy democracy.

The Erosion of Individual Agency

Identity politics reduces individuals to mere representatives of their identity groups, stripping them of their individual agency and autonomy. It assumes that individuals can only be understood through the lens of their identities, ignoring their unique experiences, beliefs, and aspirations. This reductionism denies people the opportunity to be seen as complex individuals with diverse perspectives.

The Perpetuation of Divisions

Rather than fostering unity and solidarity, identity politics perpetuates divisions among different identity groups. By emphasizing differences and grievances, it hinders the formation of common goals and shared values. This fragmentation weakens social movements and impedes progress towards a more inclusive society.

Conclusion

Identity politics has devolved into a paradoxical ideology that creates hierarchies of oppression. The focus on individual identities rather than shared humanity undermines efforts to achieve true equality and social justice. It is crucial to recognize the dangers of this ideology and seek alternative approaches that promote inclusivity, empathy, and understanding without perpetuating divisions.

Chapter 8: The Myth of Cultural Appropriation: Identity Politics and the Attack on Cultural Exchange

One of the most alarming aspects of identity politics is its attack on cultural exchange through the concept of cultural appropriation.

Cultural appropriation is the idea that members of one culture should not adopt or use elements from another culture. According to proponents of this concept, doing so is a form of theft and disrespect. They argue that only members of a particular culture have the right to use and benefit from their own cultural practices and traditions.

The Dangers of Cultural Appropriation

At first glance, the idea of cultural appropriation may seem harmless. After all, isn't it just about respecting and honoring different cultures? Unfortunately, the reality is far more insidious. The concept of cultural appropriation is used as a weapon to stifle creativity, limit freedom of expression, and perpetuate division among people.

By labeling certain forms of cultural exchange as appropriation, identity politics advocates create an atmosphere of fear and censorship. They argue that individuals who engage in cultural exchange are guilty of stealing from marginalized communities and perpetuating harmful stereotypes. This leads to self-censorship and stifles artistic expression.

Furthermore, the concept of cultural appropriation assumes that cultures are static and monolithic entities that can be owned by a particular group. This ignores the reality that cultures are dynamic and constantly evolving through interaction with other cultures. Cultural exchange has been a fundamental aspect of human history and has enriched societies throughout time.

The Attack on Creativity

One of the most troubling aspects of the cultural appropriation debate is its impact on creativity. By discouraging individuals from exploring and incorporating elements from different cultures, identity politics advocates limit the possibilities for artistic expression.

Artists have always drawn inspiration from a variety of sources, including different cultures. This cross-pollination of ideas and influences has led to some of the most groundbreaking and innovative works in history. However, under the ideology of cultural appropriation, artists are discouraged from exploring new ideas and are instead confined to their own cultural boundaries.

This stifling of creativity not only harms artists but also deprives society as a whole of the benefits that come from cultural exchange. It is through the exploration and blending of different cultures that new ideas and perspectives emerge, leading to greater understanding and appreciation of our shared humanity.

Perpetuating Division

Identity politics, including its stance on cultural appropriation, perpetuates division among people. By emphasizing differences and promoting a sense of ownership over culture, this ideology creates intergroup conflict that hinders social cohesion.

Rather than celebrating our shared humanity and recognizing the commonalities that exist across cultures, identity politics encourages individuals to view each other through the lens of their respective identities. This leads to a fragmented society where people are pitted against each other based on their race, gender, or other characteristics.

Furthermore, the concept of cultural appropriation assumes that cultures are homogeneous entities with clear boundaries. In reality, cultures are fluid and constantly evolving through interaction with other cultures. By discouraging cultural exchange, identity politics advocates deny individuals the opportunity to learn from each other and bridge divides.

The Importance of Cultural Exchange

Cultural exchange is a fundamental aspect of human history and has played a crucial role in the development of societies. It has allowed for the sharing of knowledge, ideas, and traditions, leading to greater understanding and appreciation of different cultures.

Through cultural exchange, individuals have the opportunity to learn from each other, challenge their own preconceptions, and broaden their perspectives. It is through this exchange that we can break down barriers and build bridges between different communities.

Rather than demonizing cultural exchange through the concept of cultural appropriation, we should encourage a more inclusive and open-minded approach. This means celebrating the diversity of our society while also recognizing our shared humanity.

Conclusion

The concept of cultural appropriation, as promoted by identity politics, is a dangerous ideology that threatens to undermine creativity, perpetuate division, and limit our ability to learn from each other. It is important that we reject this divisive ideology and instead embrace cultural exchange as a means to foster understanding and appreciation of different cultures.

By celebrating our shared humanity and recognizing the value of cultural exchange, we can create a more inclusive and harmonious society. Let us reject the myth of cultural appropriation and embrace the power of cultural exchange to enrich our lives.

Chapter 9: The Destruction of Meritocracy: How Identity Politics Undermines Achievement and Excellence

One of the most devastating consequences of identity ideology is the destruction of meritocracy, the principle that individuals should be rewarded based on their abilities and achievements rather than their identity.

The Erosion of Standards

Identity politics operates on the flawed premise that all groups should be represented equally in every field, regardless of individual merit. This misguided belief has led to a dangerous erosion of standards in our society. Instead of valuing excellence and achievement, identity politics promotes mediocrity and tokenism.

In education, for example, schools and universities are pressured to admit students based on their identity rather than their academic abilities. This not only undermines the credibility of our educational institutions but also denies deserving students the opportunity to excel. When admissions decisions are based on factors such as race or gender rather than merit, it sends a message that hard work and talent are irrelevant.

Similarly, in the workplace, identity politics has led to the implementation of diversity quotas and affirmative action policies. While these initiatives may seem well-intentioned, they ultimately undermine the principles of meritocracy. Instead of hiring or promoting individuals based on their qualifications and skills, companies are forced to prioritize diversity over excellence. This not only harms those who are more qualified but also creates a culture where mediocrity is celebrated over achievement.

The Demise of Individual Responsibility

Identity politics also erodes individual responsibility by placing blame on external factors such as systemic oppression or privilege. Instead of encouraging individuals to take control of their own lives and strive for success, identity politics fosters a victim mentality where personal agency is diminished.

By attributing success or failure solely to one's identity, identity politics removes the incentive for individuals to work hard and overcome obstacles. It perpetuates the belief that one's fate is predetermined by factors beyond their control, leading to a sense of entitlement and complacency.

Furthermore, identity politics discourages individuals from taking responsibility for their own actions and choices. Instead of holding individuals accountable for their behavior, it attributes their actions to their identity group. This not only undermines personal growth and development but also perpetuates a cycle of victimhood and blame.

The Way Forward

To preserve meritocracy and ensure a fair and just society, it is crucial that we reject the dangerous ideology of identity politics. We must prioritize individual merit and achievement over group identity, valuing excellence over mediocrity.

Education institutions should focus on providing equal opportunities for all students based on their abilities rather than their identity. Similarly, workplaces should prioritize hiring and promoting individuals based on their qualifications and skills, rather than implementing diversity quotas.

Furthermore, we must encourage personal responsibility and agency, empowering individuals to take control of their own lives and strive for success. By fostering a culture of accountability, we can break free from the victim mentality perpetuated by identity politics.

Lastly, we must protect freedom of speech and promote open dialogue. Intellectual diversity is essential for progress and innovation. By embracing differing viewpoints and engaging in respectful debate, we can challenge the status quo and ensure a society that values critical thinking.

Conclusion

The destructive nature of identity politics on meritocracy cannot be underestimated. It undermines standards, erodes individual responsibility, suppresses dissent, and ultimately threatens the very fabric of our society. It is imperative that we reject this dangerous ideology and work towards a society that values achievement and excellence above all else.

Chapter 10: The Fallacy of Safe Spaces: Identity Politics and the Censorship of Ideas

One of the most concerning aspects of identity politics is the creation of so-called safe spaces, which are meant to provide a refuge for individuals who have been historically marginalized or oppressed. However, these safe spaces often lead to the censorship of ideas and the stifling of intellectual discourse.

The concept of safe spaces originated in the feminist movement as a way to create environments where women could freely discuss their experiences without fear of judgment or harassment. While this initial intention was well-meaning, it has since evolved into something much more insidious. Safe spaces are now used as a tool to silence dissenting opinions and shield individuals from ideas that challenge their own beliefs.

The Echo Chamber Effect

One of the main problems with safe spaces is that they create echo chambers, where like-minded individuals reinforce each other's beliefs without any critical examination. When people only surround themselves with others who share their perspectives, they become less open to alternative viewpoints and less willing to engage in meaningful dialogue. This leads to intellectual stagnation and an inability to grow and learn from others.

Furthermore, safe spaces often foster an environment where individuals are afraid to express dissenting opinions for fear of being ostracized or labeled as oppressive. This stifles intellectual diversity and hinders the development of well-rounded individuals who can engage in thoughtful debate and consider multiple perspectives.

The Suppression of Free Speech

Another alarming consequence of identity politics and safe spaces is the suppression of free speech. In an effort to protect marginalized groups, certain ideas and opinions are deemed off-limits and labeled as hate speech or harmful. While it is important to protect individuals from genuine harm, the line between legitimate concerns and censorship becomes blurred in the context of safe spaces.

The danger lies in the fact that what is considered offensive or harmful can vary greatly depending on one's perspective. By allowing certain groups to dictate what can and cannot be said, we risk silencing important voices and limiting the free exchange of ideas. This not only hinders intellectual growth but also undermines the very foundation of a democratic society.

The Illusion of Safety

Perhaps the most concerning aspect of safe spaces is the false sense of security they provide. By shielding individuals from ideas that challenge their beliefs, safe spaces create an illusion of safety that ultimately hinders personal growth and resilience. In the real world, individuals will inevitably encounter differing opinions and perspectives, and it is crucial that they develop the skills to navigate these encounters in a constructive manner.

Safe spaces perpetuate a culture of victimhood, where individuals are encouraged to see themselves as perpetual victims rather than empowered agents capable of effecting change. This victim mentality not only undermines personal agency but also perpetuates a cycle of division and animosity between different identity groups.

Moving Towards Constructive Dialogue

It is important to recognize that identity politics and safe spaces are not inherently evil or without merit. They have emerged as a response to genuine injustices and inequalities in our society. However, it is crucial that we critically examine the unintended consequences of these ideologies and work towards creating environments that foster constructive dialogue rather than stifling it.

Instead of retreating into safe spaces, we should encourage individuals to engage with diverse perspectives and challenge their own beliefs. This requires creating spaces where respectful and open-minded dialogue can take place, free from the fear of judgment or harassment. It also requires individuals to develop the skills necessary to navigate difficult conversations and engage in productive debate.

Conclusion

While the intentions behind identity politics and safe spaces may be noble, it is important to critically examine the dangers and problems that arise from these ideologies. The creation of echo chambers, the suppression of free speech, and the illusion of safety all hinder intellectual growth and perpetuate division. By moving towards constructive dialogue and fostering environments that encourage open-mindedness and critical thinking, we can work towards a more inclusive and intellectually vibrant society.

Chapter 11: The Manipulation of History: Identity Politics and the Rewriting of the Past

The Power of Narrative

History is not just a collection of facts and events; it is the story we tell ourselves about who we are as a society. It shapes our understanding of the past and influences our present and future. Identity politics understands this power and exploits it to further its own agenda.

By rewriting history through the lens of identity, proponents of this ideology seek to create a new narrative that supports their worldview. They cherry-pick historical events and reinterpret them in a way that reinforces their claims of victimhood and oppression. This selective approach to history not only distorts the truth but also erases the complexity and nuance that is inherent in any historical account.

The Erasure of Heroes

One of the most alarming consequences of identity politics' manipulation of history is the erasure of heroes. Figures who were once celebrated for their contributions to society are now vilified based on their perceived shortcomings or associations with groups deemed oppressive by identity ideologues.

For example, historical figures like George Washington and Thomas Jefferson, who played pivotal roles in the founding of the United States, are now portrayed as nothing more than slave-owning oppressors. Their accomplishments and contributions are overshadowed by their flaws, effectively erasing their positive impact on society.

This rewriting of history not only diminishes the achievements of these individuals but also undermines the foundations of our society. By erasing our heroes, identity politics seeks to delegitimize the very institutions and values that have made our society prosperous and free.

The Distortion of Oppression

Identity politics also distorts the historical reality of oppression. While it is undeniable that various groups have faced discrimination and injustice throughout history, identity politics exaggerates and simplifies these narratives to fit its own agenda.

By portraying all historical events as a struggle between oppressors and oppressed, identity politics ignores the complexity of human history. It reduces individuals to mere representatives of their identity groups, erasing their agency and individuality. This oversimplification not only distorts the past but also hinders our ability to learn from it.

The Danger of Victimhood

Identity politics thrives on victimhood. By perpetuating a narrative of victimization, it creates a sense of collective grievance among certain groups, fostering division and resentment.

This victimhood mentality not only distorts historical realities but also hinders progress. Instead of focusing on solutions and working towards a more inclusive society, identity politics encourages individuals to see themselves as perpetual victims, forever oppressed by an unjust system.

The Threat to Free Speech

Perhaps one of the most concerning aspects of identity politics' manipulation of history is its impact on free speech. By controlling the narrative and silencing dissenting voices, proponents of this ideology create an environment where alternative viewpoints are suppressed.

Those who dare to question or challenge the prevailing narrative are labeled as bigots or oppressors, effectively shutting down any meaningful dialogue. This stifling of free speech not only undermines the principles of democracy but also hinders our ability to learn from history and grow as a society.

Conclusion

The manipulation of history by identity politics is a dangerous trend that threatens the very foundations of our society. By rewriting the past, erasing heroes, distorting oppression, fostering victimhood, and suppressing free speech, this ideology seeks to reshape our collective narrative in a way that serves its own agenda.

It is crucial that we remain vigilant and critical of the narratives presented to us. We must strive for a more nuanced understanding of history, one that acknowledges both the triumphs and the failures of our past. Only through an honest and inclusive examination of history can we hope to build a better future for all.

Chapter 12: The Danger of Tribalism: How Identity Politics Fuels Divisions and Hostility

This chapter aims to shed light on the dangers of tribalism that arise from identity politics.

The Erosion of Individuality

Identity politics undermines the very essence of individuality. By reducing individuals to mere representatives of their identity group, it erases their unique experiences, talents, and aspirations. This erasure denies people the opportunity to be seen and valued for who they truly are.

Furthermore, identity politics perpetuates a victimhood mentality that discourages personal responsibility and agency. It fosters a culture where individuals are encouraged to blame external factors for their struggles rather than taking ownership of their lives. This not only hinders personal growth but also perpetuates a cycle of dependency on external validation and support.

The Weaponization of Identity

Identity politics has also led to the weaponization of identity. In an increasingly polarized society, individuals and groups exploit their identities as a means to gain power and control. They use accusations of oppression or victimhood as weapons to silence dissenting voices and stifle free speech.

This weaponization of identity creates an environment where honest conversations about important issues become nearly impossible. People fear expressing their opinions for fear of being labeled as bigots or oppressors. As a result, meaningful dialogue is replaced by virtue signaling and performative activism.

The Illusion of Unity

Ironically, while identity politics claims to champion diversity and inclusivity, it ultimately undermines these ideals. By emphasizing group identities over individuality, it perpetuates divisions based on immutable characteristics rather than fostering genuine understanding and empathy.

Identity politics creates a false sense of unity within identity groups while simultaneously deepening the divisions between them. It encourages individuals to view those outside their group as adversaries rather than potential allies. This tribalistic mindset hampers progress towards a more inclusive and harmonious society.

Moving Beyond Identity Politics

To overcome the dangers of identity politics, we must shift our focus towards a more inclusive and holistic approach. We must recognize that individuals are complex beings with multifaceted identities that cannot be reduced to a single characteristic.

We must foster a culture that values individuality, encourages critical thinking, and promotes open dialogue. This requires creating spaces where diverse perspectives can be heard and respected, even if they challenge prevailing narratives.

By moving beyond the limitations of identity politics, we can build bridges of understanding and empathy. We can work towards a society where individuals are seen and valued for their unique qualities rather than being judged solely based on their group identities.

Conclusion

Identity politics, with its emphasis on group identities and the prioritization of certain characteristics over others, has fueled divisions and hostility among individuals and communities. It has created a culture of tribalism that stifles critical thinking, erodes individuality, and hampers progress towards a more inclusive society.

To overcome these dangers, we must reject the reductionist approach of identity politics and embrace a more inclusive and holistic perspective. Only by recognizing the complexity of human beings and fostering genuine understanding can we hope to build a society free from the shackles of tribalism.

Chapter 13: The Illusion of Equality: Identity Politics and the Pursuit of Equity at All Costs

Identity politics discourages personal responsibility and agency. It tells individuals that their success or failure is determined solely by their group identity and that they have no control over their own lives. This mindset is not only disempowering but also undermines the principles of meritocracy and individual achievement.

The Illusion of Equality

One of the most dangerous aspects of identity politics is its false promise of equality. While it claims to fight for equal rights and opportunities for all, it actually perpetuates a system of inequality and division. By prioritizing certain groups over others, identity politics creates a hierarchy where some voices are deemed more valuable than others.

This hierarchy is based on the flawed notion that certain groups are inherently oppressed and others are inherently privileged. It ignores the complexities and diversity within each group, reducing individuals to mere stereotypes. In doing so, identity politics erases the unique experiences and perspectives of individuals, further marginalizing those who do not fit neatly into predefined categories.

The Way Forward

It is crucial that we recognize the dangers posed by identity politics and work towards a more inclusive and equitable society. This does not mean ignoring or dismissing the legitimate struggles faced by marginalized groups, but rather finding common ground and promoting individual rights and freedoms.

We must reject the divisive rhetoric of identity politics and instead focus on the principles that unite us as human beings. We must recognize that true equality can only be achieved when we treat each other as individuals, not as representatives of a particular group.

By embracing a more inclusive and nuanced approach, we can move beyond the limitations of identity politics and work towards a society where everyone has an equal opportunity to succeed. It is time to break free from the illusion of equality that identity politics perpetuates and strive for a future where individuality and merit are valued above all else.

Chapter 14: The Silencing Effect on Education: How Identity Politics Stifles Intellectual Growth

In recent years, identity politics has infiltrated every aspect of our society, including our educational institutions. What was once a place for open dialogue and intellectual growth has now become a breeding ground for the silencing effect of identity ideology. This chapter will explore how identity politics stifles intellectual growth in education and the dangerous consequences that arise as a result.

The Rise of Identity Politics in Education

Identity politics, rooted in the belief that one's identity is the most important aspect of their existence, has gained significant traction in educational institutions. The focus on individual identities, such as race, gender, and sexuality, has led to a shift away from objective learning and critical thinking.

Instead of encouraging students to engage in rigorous academic discourse and challenge their own beliefs, identity politics promotes a culture of victimhood and oppression. Students are taught to view themselves as victims or oppressors based on their immutable characteristics, rather than as individuals capable of independent thought.

The Silencing Effect on Free Speech

One of the most alarming consequences of identity politics in education is the silencing effect it has on free speech. In an environment where certain ideas are deemed offensive or oppressive based on the identity of the speaker, students are discouraged from expressing dissenting opinions or engaging in open debate.

This stifling of free speech not only hinders intellectual growth but also creates a belief silo where only certain perspectives are allowed to be heard. Students who hold different viewpoints are ostracized and labeled as bigots or oppressors, further discouraging them from expressing their thoughts.

The Erosion of Critical Thinking

Identity politics also erodes critical thinking skills, as students are taught to accept certain ideas without question. Instead of analyzing arguments and evidence, students are encouraged to rely on their personal experiences and emotions as the ultimate authority.

This lack of critical thinking leads to a narrow-mindedness that inhibits intellectual growth. Students become less willing to consider alternative viewpoints or engage in thoughtful debate, as they have been conditioned to believe that their own experiences are the only valid perspective.

The Dangers of Herd Mentality

Identity politics in education also fosters a dangerous culture of 'her mentality'. Students are encouraged to align themselves with specific identity groups and view those outside of their group as enemies or oppressors.

This tribalistic mentality not only hinders intellectual growth but also perpetuates division and animosity among students. Instead of fostering a sense of unity and understanding, identity politics creates an us versus them mentality that further polarizes society.

The Loss of Intellectual Diversity

Perhaps the most detrimental consequence of identity politics in education is the loss of intellectual diversity. When certain ideas are deemed unacceptable or offensive based on the identity of the speaker, a wide range of perspectives is silenced.

This homogenization of thought not only limits intellectual growth but also hinders innovation and progress. Without a diversity of ideas, students are deprived of the opportunity to engage in meaningful dialogue and challenge their own beliefs.

Conclusion

Identity politics has had a detrimental effect on education, stifling intellectual growth and hindering the development of critical thinking skills. The silencing effect it has on free speech, erosion of critical thinking, dangers of conformity, and loss of intellectual diversity are all alarming consequences that must be addressed.

If we are to foster an environment of intellectual growth and open dialogue, we must reject the stifling nature of identity politics in education. It is only through the free exchange of ideas and a commitment to intellectual diversity that we can truly expand our knowledge and understanding of the world.

Chapter 15: The Threat to Individuality: Identity Politics and the Loss of Personal Autonomy

Introduction

In this chapter, I explore the dangers and problems associated with identity politics and its potential to undermine personal autonomy.

The Tyranny of Identity

Identity politics operates on the premise that an individual's identity is determined solely by their race, gender, sexual orientation, or other group affiliations. It reduces complex individuals to mere representatives of these groups, erasing their individuality and uniqueness. By prioritizing group identity over personal autonomy, identity politics creates a dangerous environment where conformity is rewarded and independent thought is discouraged.

The Erosion of Personal Responsibility

Identity politics also undermines personal responsibility by shifting the blame for an individual's circumstances onto external factors such as systemic oppression or privilege. While acknowledging the existence of societal inequalities is important, identity politics takes it to an extreme by absolving individuals of any responsibility for their own actions and choices. This erodes personal autonomy and fosters a culture of victimhood, where individuals are encouraged to see themselves as passive recipients of their circumstances rather than active agents capable of shaping their own lives.

The Loss of Intellectual Diversity

Identity politics promotes a narrow view of the world, where individuals are defined solely by their group identities. This leads to a loss of intellectual diversity, as different perspectives and ideas are dismissed based on the identity of the person expressing them. The focus on group identity over individual thought stifles creativity and innovation, hindering progress and limiting our ability to solve complex problems.

The Threat to Personal Autonomy

Perhaps the most significant danger posed by identity politics is its threat to personal autonomy. By reducing individuals to mere representatives of their group identities, this ideology denies us the freedom to define ourselves on our own terms. Our identities become predetermined by societal expectations and norms, leaving little room for self-discovery and personal growth.

Conclusion

Identity politics presents a clear and present danger to individuality and personal autonomy. By prioritizing group identity over individuality, suppressing dissent, eroding personal responsibility, limiting intellectual diversity, and threatening personal autonomy, this ideology undermines the very foundations of a free society. It is crucial that we recognize these dangers and actively resist the encroachment of identity politics in order to preserve our ability to think, act, and be unique individuals.

Chapter 16: The Dangers of Group Rights Over Individual Rights in Identity Politics

In this chapter, I will explore the alarming consequences of prioritizing group rights over individual rights in identity politics.

The Erosion of Individual Autonomy

One of the fundamental principles of a liberal democracy is the protection of individual autonomy. This means that individuals have the right to make choices about their own lives, free from interference or coercion. However, identity politics undermines this principle by emphasizing group identities over individual agency.

When group rights take precedence, individuals are reduced to mere representatives of their identity category. Their thoughts, beliefs, and actions are expected to align with the collective interests of their group. This erodes individual autonomy and stifles dissenting voices within marginalized communities.

The Tyranny of Majority

Identity politics often operates on the assumption that certain groups are inherently oppressed while others are privileged. While it is crucial to address historical injustices and systemic inequalities, the focus on group rights can lead to a dangerous form of majority tyranny.

When group rights become the primary concern, it opens the door for majority groups to assert their own interests at the expense of minority groups. This can result in policies that perpetuate discrimination and marginalization under the guise of rectifying historical injustices. In essence, identity politics risks replacing one form of oppression with another.

Divisiveness and Polarization

Identity politics thrives on the notion of collective victimhood and oppression. It encourages individuals to view themselves primarily through the lens of their group identity, fostering an us versus them mentality. This divisive rhetoric undermines social cohesion and hinders meaningful dialogue.

By prioritizing group rights, identity politics creates an environment where individuals are pitted against each other based on their identities. This not only perpetuates stereotypes and prejudices but also hampers efforts to build bridges and find common ground.

The Loss of Individual Merit

Identity politics places significant emphasis on group representation and diversity quotas. While diversity is undoubtedly important, it should not come at the expense of individual merit and qualifications.

When group rights are prioritized over individual rights, it can lead to a devaluation of individual achievements. Instead of recognizing individuals for their skills, talents, and hard work, identity politics promotes a system where group membership becomes the primary determinant of success or failure.

Conclusion

While identity politics may claim to fight for equality and justice, its focus on group rights over individual rights poses significant dangers. The erosion of individual autonomy, the tyranny of majority, divisiveness and polarization, the suppression of free speech, and the loss of individual merit are just a few of the alarming consequences.

To build a truly inclusive and just society, we must recognize the importance of both group and individual rights. By striking a balance between the two, we can ensure that no one is marginalized or oppressed while preserving the fundamental principles of individual autonomy and freedom.

Chapter 17: The Rise of Identity Extremism: How Identity Politics Breeds Radicalism

In recent years, we have witnessed a disturbing trend in our society - the rise of identity extremism. Identity politics, once seen as a means to promote inclusivity and social justice, has now become a breeding ground for radicalism and division. This chapter aims to shed light on the dangers and problems associated with identity ideology, highlighting how it has led to the emergence of extreme factions within various communities.

The Fragmentation of Society

Identity politics, at its core, seeks to prioritize the experiences and perspectives of marginalized groups. While this may seem like a noble goal, it has inadvertently led to the fragmentation of society. By encouraging individuals to view themselves primarily through the lens of their identity, we have created an us versus them mentality that fosters division rather than unity.

This fragmentation is particularly evident on college campuses, where students are increasingly being taught to view the world through the narrow prism of their own identity. Instead of fostering open dialogue and intellectual exploration, this approach stifles free speech and promotes an ideological enclave. Students are discouraged from engaging with ideas that challenge their preconceived notions, leading to intellectual stagnation and an inability to critically analyze complex issues.

The Rise of Identity-Based Violence

Perhaps the most alarming consequence of identity extremism is the rise of identity-based violence. When individuals are taught to view themselves primarily through the lens of their identity, it becomes easier to dehumanize those who belong to different groups.

We have seen this play out in various forms, from extremist groups advocating for violence against perceived oppressors to acts of domestic terrorism committed in the name of identity-based ideologies. The dangerous combination of radicalization and identity politics has created a fertile ground for extremism to flourish.

The Erosion of Individuality

Identity extremism also poses a threat to individuality. By encouraging individuals to define themselves solely based on their identity, we risk reducing complex human beings to mere stereotypes. This reductionist approach undermines the richness and diversity of human experiences, limiting our understanding and appreciation for the complexity of individual lives.

Furthermore, this emphasis on identity can lead to a sense of victimhood and entitlement, where individuals believe they are owed certain privileges or protections solely based on their identity. This erodes personal responsibility and undermines the principles of meritocracy and equal opportunity.

Conclusion

While the initial intentions behind identity politics may have been noble, it is clear that the ideology has taken a dangerous turn. The rise of identity extremism threatens to further divide our society, suppress dissenting voices, and perpetuate violence in the name of identity-based ideologies.

It is crucial that we recognize the dangers and problems associated with identity politics and work towards a more inclusive and nuanced approach. We must foster open dialogue, encourage critical thinking, and promote a society that values individuality while also recognizing the importance of collective progress.

Chapter 18: The Commodification of Victimhood: Identity Politics and the Marketplace of Grievances

Introduction

In recent years, identity politics has gained significant traction in public discourse. Advocates argue that it is a necessary tool for addressing historical injustices and promoting social equality. However, beneath the surface, there lies a dangerous trend: the commodification of victimhood. Identity politics has transformed into a marketplace of grievances, where individuals compete for recognition and power based on their perceived victim status. This chapter explores the perils of this phenomenon and its implications for society.

The Marketplace of Grievances

In the marketplace of grievances, victimhood is no longer seen as an unfortunate circumstance but rather as a valuable commodity. People now vie for attention and sympathy by exaggerating or fabricating their experiences of oppression. This competition creates an environment where victimhood is not only celebrated but also rewarded.

Social media platforms have become breeding grounds for this phenomenon. Users engage in performative displays of victimhood, sharing personal stories that often lack veracity or context. The more sensational the story, the greater the chance of gaining followers, likes, and shares.

The Dangers of Commodifying Victimhood

The commodification of victimhood poses several dangers to society. Firstly, it undermines the credibility of genuine victims and their struggles. When everyone claims to be a victim, it becomes increasingly difficult to discern truth from fiction. This dilution of victimhood erodes public trust and hampers efforts to address real injustices.

Secondly, the marketplace of grievances perpetuates a culture of victimhood and entitlement. Individuals are encouraged to view themselves primarily through the lens of their perceived oppression, rather than as individuals with agency and resilience. This victim mentality stifles personal growth and perpetuates a cycle of dependency on external validation.

Furthermore, the commodification of victimhood fuels division and polarization within society. As different groups compete for recognition, they often engage in a zero-sum game where one group's gain is seen as another's loss. This creates an environment of hostility and animosity, hindering any possibility of genuine dialogue and understanding.

The Impact on Democracy

Identity politics, in its current form, poses a significant threat to democratic values. The focus on individual identity fragments society into isolated groups, each vying for their own interests. This fragmentation weakens the collective bonds that hold a democracy together.

Moreover, the marketplace of grievances encourages a culture of censorship and self-censorship. Individuals fear expressing dissenting opinions or engaging in open debate for fear of being labeled oppressors or insensitive. This stifling of free speech undermines the very foundation upon which democracy thrives.

Conclusion

While identity politics initially aimed to address historical injustices, it has devolved into a dangerous marketplace of grievances. The commodification of victimhood undermines genuine struggles, perpetuates a culture of entitlement, fuels division, and threatens democratic values. It is imperative that we recognize these dangers and strive for a more inclusive and nuanced approach to social justice.

Chapter 19: The Polarization of Society: How Identity Politics Deepens Divisions

Introduction

In this chapter, I will explore how identity politics polarizes society and why we must be wary of its consequences.

The Us vs. Them Mentality

One of the most dangerous aspects of identity politics is its tendency to foster an us vs. them mentality. By emphasizing differences and promoting the idea that certain groups are oppressed while others are privileged, identity politics creates an environment where individuals are pitted against each other based on their identities. This not only perpetuates division but also hinders meaningful dialogue and cooperation.

Instead of encouraging unity and understanding, identity politics encourages people to view others solely through the lens of their identity. It reduces complex individuals to mere representatives of their group, ignoring their unique experiences and perspectives. This narrow-minded approach prevents us from seeing each other as individuals with shared humanity and common goals.

The Suppression of Dissenting Voices

Identity politics also poses a threat to free speech and intellectual diversity. In its quest for social justice, this ideology often silences dissenting voices by labeling them as oppressive or privileged. Those who dare to question or challenge the prevailing narrative are accused of being insensitive or even bigoted.

This suppression of dissenting voices not only stifles intellectual debate but also prevents us from critically examining the ideas and assumptions underlying identity politics. By shutting down alternative perspectives, we risk creating a homogeneous mindset where only one viewpoint is allowed, leading to a dangerous lack of intellectual diversity and the erosion of democratic values.

The Balkanization of Society

Identity politics further exacerbates divisions by promoting the balkanization of society. Instead of fostering a sense of shared national identity, this ideology encourages individuals to identify primarily with their specific group. This fragmentation weakens our collective bonds and undermines social cohesion.

When people are encouraged to prioritize their group identity over their shared identity as citizens, it becomes increasingly difficult to find common ground and work towards common goals. This fragmentation not only hinders progress but also creates fertile ground for animosity and conflict between different groups.

The Erosion of Meritocracy

Identity politics also poses a threat to meritocracy, the principle that individuals should be rewarded based on their abilities and achievements rather than their identities. By placing undue emphasis on group identities, this ideology undermines the idea that individuals should be judged on their merits.

When hiring decisions, college admissions, or any other form of evaluation are based on identity rather than qualifications, it not only undermines the principles of fairness and equal opportunity but also perpetuates a system where individuals are valued solely for their group membership. This erosion of meritocracy not only harms individuals who may be overlooked due to their qualifications but also undermines societal trust in institutions.

The Way Forward

To address the polarization caused by identity politics, we must strive for a more inclusive and nuanced approach to social justice. Instead of focusing solely on group identities, we should recognize the complexity and diversity within each individual. By fostering empathy, understanding, and dialogue, we can bridge the divides that identity politics has created.

Furthermore, we must promote intellectual diversity and protect free speech. Allowing for a wide range of perspectives and encouraging open debate is essential for a healthy democracy. By embracing dissenting voices and challenging our own assumptions, we can foster a society that values critical thinking and intellectual growth.

Lastly, we must reaffirm the importance of meritocracy and equal opportunity. While it is crucial to address historical injustices and systemic inequalities, we must do so without sacrificing the principles of fairness and individual achievement. By creating a society that rewards individuals based on their abilities rather than their identities, we can build a more just and cohesive future.

Conclusion

Identity politics may have started with good intentions, but its consequences are far from positive. By deepening divisions, suppressing dissenting voices, promoting balkanization, and eroding meritocracy, this ideology threatens to tear our society apart. It is up to us to recognize these dangers and work towards a more inclusive and united future.

In today's society, identity politics has become a pervasive and dangerous force that threatens to undermine the very foundations of our democracy. From the classroom to the boardroom, from the media to the government, identity ideology has infiltrated every aspect of our lives, dividing us into ever smaller and more polarized groups.

Chapter 20: The Danger of Identity Essentialism: How Identity Politics Reduces People to Their Identities

Identity politics has become an increasingly pervasive force in our society, shaping the way we view ourselves and others. While the intention behind identity politics may be to promote inclusivity and equality, it has inadvertently created a dangerous environment where individuals are reduced to their identities, leading to division, polarization, and the erosion of individuality.

The Reduction of Individuality

Identity politics reduces individuals to mere representatives of their respective groups. It ignores the complexity and diversity within each person, reducing them to a single dimension defined by their race, gender, or sexual orientation.

This reduction of individuality is dangerous because it denies people the opportunity to be seen as unique individuals with their own thoughts, beliefs, and experiences. Instead, they are forced into predefined boxes that limit their potential for growth and self-expression.

The Erosion of Dialogue

Identity politics has also led to the erosion of meaningful dialogue. Instead of engaging in thoughtful conversations and debates, individuals are encouraged to retreat into their identity groups, where dissenting opinions are met with hostility and accusations of bigotry.

This lack of dialogue stifles intellectual growth and prevents the exchange of ideas. It creates an echo chamber where individuals are only exposed to viewpoints that align with their own, further entrenching their beliefs and widening the divide between different identity groups.

The Polarization of Society

Identity politics has contributed to the polarization of society. By dividing people into distinct identity groups, it fosters an us versus them mentality that perpetuates conflict and animosity.

Instead of working towards common goals and finding shared values, identity politics encourages individuals to view others as adversaries. This not only hinders progress but also deepens societal divisions, making it increasingly difficult to find common ground and build bridges between different communities.

The Danger of Identity Essentialism

Perhaps the most alarming aspect of identity politics is its tendency towards essentialism. Essentialism is the belief that certain characteristics or qualities are inherent to a particular identity group.

Essentialism reduces individuals to stereotypes and perpetuates harmful generalizations. It assumes that all members of a particular group think, act, and believe in the same way, erasing the diversity and complexity within each group.

This dangerous form of essentialism not only reinforces stereotypes but also denies individuals agency over their own lives. It assumes that their identities dictate their beliefs and actions, stripping them of their autonomy and individuality.

The Path Forward

To overcome the dangers of identity politics, we must shift our focus from divisive identity essentialism to a more inclusive and nuanced understanding of individuals.

We must recognize that while identities are an important part of who we are, they do not define us entirely. We are complex beings with a multitude of experiences, beliefs, and aspirations that extend beyond our identities.

By embracing individuality and fostering dialogue that transcends identity boundaries, we can create a society that celebrates diversity while also recognizing our shared humanity. Only then can we move towards a more inclusive and equitable future for all.

Chapter 21: The Threat to Democracy: Identity Politics and the Erosion of Civic Engagement

The Erosion of Civic Engagement

Identity politics also poses a significant threat to civic engagement. When individuals prioritize their group identity above their shared identity as citizens, they become less invested in the well-being of their communities and the democratic process as a whole.

In a healthy democracy, citizens actively participate in civic life, engaging in activities such as voting, volunteering, and community organizing. However, identity politics encourages individuals to view these activities through the lens of their group interests rather than the collective good. This leads to a decline in civic engagement and a weakening of democratic institutions.

The Path Forward

To safeguard our democracy from the dangers of identity politics, we must prioritize individuality over group identity. We must recognize that each person is more than the sum of their characteristics and that our shared humanity should unite us, rather than divide us.

We must also foster an environment where diverse perspectives are welcomed and respected. This means encouraging open dialogue, promoting intellectual diversity, and challenging the echo chambers created by identity politics.

Furthermore, we must reaffirm the importance of free speech as a cornerstone of democracy. We must defend the right of individuals to express their opinions, even when those opinions may be uncomfortable or unpopular. Only through the free exchange of ideas can we arrive at informed decisions and build a stronger society.

Lastly, we must reinvigorate civic engagement by emphasizing our shared responsibilities as citizens. By focusing on the common good rather than narrow group interests, we can rebuild trust, cooperation, and a sense of community.

Conclusion

Identity politics poses a grave threat to our democracy. Its emphasis on group identities over individual identities fosters a collective mindset, tribalism, and the suppression of free speech. It erodes civic engagement and weakens democratic institutions. To preserve our democracy, we must reject this dangerous ideology and embrace a vision of society that values individuality, diversity, and the common good.

Chapter 22: The Illusion of Inclusivity: How Identity Politics Excludes Dissenting Voices

This chapter aims to shed light on how identity politics can inadvertently exclude dissenting voices, stifling meaningful dialogue and impeding progress.

The Suppression of Dissenting Voices

Identity politics, in its quest for inclusivity, often ends up excluding those who do not conform to the prevailing narrative. Dissenting voices, even from within marginalized communities, are often dismissed or attacked for challenging the status quo. This exclusionary approach undermines the very principles of diversity and inclusivity that identity politics claims to champion.

Moreover, the suppression of dissenting voices can have severe consequences for individuals who dare to question the prevailing orthodoxy. They may face social ostracization, professional repercussions, or even threats to their personal safety. This creates a chilling effect on free speech and discourages open dialogue, hindering progress and perpetuating a culture of fear.

The Limitations of Identity as a Sole Determinant

Identity politics places an undue emphasis on immutable characteristics as the sole determinant of an individual's experiences and perspectives. While acknowledging the impact of identity is crucial, it is equally important to recognize that individuals are complex beings shaped by a multitude of factors beyond their identity.

Reducing individuals to their identities oversimplifies their experiences and overlooks the diversity within marginalized communities. It fails to account for differences in socioeconomic status, education, cultural background, and personal values that shape an individual's worldview. By solely focusing on identity, we risk perpetuating stereotypes and denying individuals agency over their own lives.

Embracing a More Inclusive Approach

To address the dangers and problems associated with identity politics, we must strive for a more inclusive approach that values diverse perspectives and encourages open dialogue. This requires moving beyond the confines of identity and embracing a broader understanding of human experiences.

We must create spaces where dissenting voices are welcomed and respected, fostering an environment that encourages critical thinking and intellectual growth. By engaging in respectful dialogue, we can challenge our own assumptions, broaden our perspectives, and work towards solutions that benefit all members of society.

Conclusion

While identity politics initially aimed to address historical injustices, it has inadvertently created a framework that excludes dissenting voices. By fostering uniformity of thought, suppressing alternative perspectives, and oversimplifying individuals' experiences, identity politics hampers meaningful dialogue and impedes progress. It is crucial to recognize the limitations of identity as a sole determinant and embrace a more inclusive approach that values diversity of thought. Only then can we truly create a society that is inclusive, equitable, and just for all.

Chapter 23: The Weaponization of Empathy in Identity Politics

The Illusion of Empathy

One of the most insidious aspects of identity politics is its use of empathy as a weapon. Empathy, the ability to understand and share the feelings of another person, is a fundamental aspect of human nature. It allows us to connect with others on a deep emotional level and fosters compassion and understanding.

However, identity politics distorts this natural human instinct by encouraging individuals to prioritize empathy for those who share their own identity while dismissing or even demonizing those who do not. This selective empathy creates an us versus them mentality that erodes social cohesion and undermines the very foundations of a healthy society.

When empathy is weaponized in identity politics, it becomes a tool for enforcing conformity within these social groups. Those who deviate from the accepted narrative are labeled as traitors or sellouts, effectively silencing any dissenting voices and perpetuating a dangerous echo chamber.

The Suppression of Individuality

Identity politics also poses a threat to individuality. By reducing individuals to a set of predetermined characteristics, it denies the complexity and uniqueness of each person. It discourages individuals from exploring their own interests, talents, and passions, instead pressuring them to conform to the expectations of their identity group.

This suppression of individuality is particularly harmful to marginalized communities. Instead of empowering individuals to rise above their circumstances and pursue their own dreams and aspirations, identity politics confines them to a narrow set of predefined roles and expectations.

The Erosion of Meritocracy

Identity politics also undermines the principles of meritocracy. Meritocracy is the idea that individuals should be rewarded based on their abilities and achievements rather than their identity. It is a cornerstone of a fair and just society.

However, identity politics seeks to replace meritocracy with a system that rewards individuals based on their group identity rather than their individual accomplishments. This not only undermines the motivation and drive of individuals but also perpetuates a cycle of victimhood and entitlement.

The Divisiveness of Identity Politics

Perhaps the most alarming aspect of identity politics is its inherent divisiveness. By encouraging individuals to view themselves primarily through the lens of their identity, it creates an us versus them mentality that pits different groups against each other.

This divisiveness not only hinders meaningful dialogue and understanding but also fosters animosity and hostility between different groups. It erodes the social fabric of our society and undermines the very foundations of a harmonious and inclusive community.

Conclusion

The weaponization of empathy in identity politics is a dangerous and destructive force. It distorts our natural human instinct for empathy, promotes a hive mind, suppresses individuality, erodes meritocracy, and fosters divisiveness. It is imperative that we recognize these dangers and work towards a society that values empathy for all individuals, regardless of their identity.

Chapter 24: The Danger of Moral Relativism in Identity Politics

Identity politics, the practice of organizing political movements around specific social identities, has gained significant traction in recent years. While the intentions behind this movement may be noble, there is a dangerous undercurrent that threatens to undermine the very fabric of our society. This undercurrent is moral relativism, the belief that there are no objective moral truths and that all moral judgments are subjective and relative.

Moral relativism has seeped into identity politics through the lens of intersectionality, a concept that recognizes the interconnected nature of social identities and the ways in which they intersect to create unique experiences of oppression and privilege. While intersectionality can be a valuable tool for understanding and addressing systemic inequalities, it becomes problematic when it is used to justify moral relativism.

The Slippery Slope of Moral Relativism

Moral relativism opens the door to a dangerous slippery slope where all moral judgments become equally valid. This means that any action or belief, no matter how harmful or oppressive, can be justified as long as it aligns with someone's subjective experience of their identity. This undermines the very notion of universal human rights and allows for the perpetuation of injustice under the guise of individual autonomy.

For example, if someone believes that their identity as a member of an oppressed group justifies violence against those they perceive as oppressors, then according to moral relativism, their actions cannot be condemned. This creates a dangerous precedent where violence and oppression become acceptable as long as they are carried out by those who claim victimhood.

The Erosion of Objective Truth

Moral relativism also erodes the concept of objective truth, which is essential for a functioning society. Without a shared understanding of what is right and wrong, it becomes impossible to hold individuals and institutions accountable for their actions. This leads to a breakdown in trust and the erosion of social cohesion.

In an identity politics framework that embraces moral relativism, any attempt to challenge or question someone's subjective experience of their identity is seen as an act of oppression. This stifles debate and critical thinking, as any dissenting opinion is dismissed as invalid or even harmful. The result is an echo chamber where only one perspective is allowed, leading to the suppression of diverse voices and the loss of intellectual rigor.

The Need for Objective Moral Standards

To address the dangers posed by moral relativism in identity politics, we must reassert the importance of objective moral standards. While it is crucial to recognize and address systemic inequalities, we cannot allow these efforts to devolve into a free-for-all where any action or belief can be justified.

Objective moral standards provide a framework for evaluating the ethical implications of our actions and beliefs. They allow us to hold individuals and institutions accountable for their behavior and ensure that justice is served. Without these standards, we risk descending into chaos and moral nihilism.

Conclusion

The danger of moral relativism in identity politics cannot be overstated. It undermines the very foundations of our society by eroding objective truth, fostering common consent, and justifying harmful actions. To preserve the values we hold dear, we must reject moral relativism and embrace the importance of objective moral standards.

Chapter 25: The Erosion of Personal Agency in Identity Politics

One of the most concerning consequences of identity politics is the erosion of personal agency.

The Power of Identity

Identity is a fundamental aspect of human existence. It shapes our beliefs, values, and experiences, providing us with a sense of belonging and purpose. However, when identity becomes the sole lens through which we view ourselves and others, it can lead to a dangerous reductionism that undermines personal agency.

Identity politics often encourages individuals to define themselves primarily by their race, gender, sexual orientation, or other immutable characteristics. While acknowledging and celebrating diversity is important, reducing individuals to these categories oversimplifies their complex identities and limits their potential for growth and self-determination.

The Tyranny of Groupthink

Identity politics fosters a culture of groupthink, where individuals are expected to conform to the beliefs and values associated with their identity group. This pressure to conform stifles dissenting voices and discourages critical thinking.

When personal agency is eroded in this way, individuals become mere representatives of their identity group rather than autonomous beings with unique perspectives and experiences. This not only undermines individuality but also hampers progress by discouraging diverse viewpoints and innovative ideas.

The Victimhood Narrative

Identity politics often promotes a victimhood narrative, where individuals are encouraged to view themselves as oppressed and marginalized solely based on their identity. While it is essential to address systemic inequalities and injustices, perpetuating a victimhood narrative can be detrimental to personal agency.

When individuals are constantly told that they are victims, they may internalize this narrative and believe that their actions and choices have little impact on their lives. This mindset robs individuals of their agency, making them passive recipients of societal forces rather than active participants in shaping their own destinies.

The Danger of Identity Essentialism

Identity politics often promotes essentialism, the belief that certain characteristics or experiences are inherent to specific identity groups. While recognizing shared experiences can be empowering, essentialism can lead to a dangerous homogenization of identities.

When individuals are reduced to a set of predetermined characteristics based on their identity, it becomes difficult for them to break free from societal expectations and stereotypes. This erodes personal agency by limiting the range of possibilities for self-expression and self-determination.

Reclaiming Personal Agency

To counteract the erosion of personal agency in identity politics, it is crucial to promote a more nuanced understanding of identity that recognizes the complexity and individuality of each person.

Encouraging individuals to explore multiple aspects of their identity beyond their immutable characteristics can help foster a sense of personal agency. Emphasizing the importance of individual choices and actions can empower individuals to take control of their lives and shape their own narratives.

Furthermore, promoting dialogue and open-mindedness within identity groups can help challenge social conformity and encourage diverse perspectives. By embracing intellectual diversity, we can create spaces where personal agency is valued and individuals are free to express their unique viewpoints.

Conclusion

While identity politics may have emerged with good intentions, it is essential to recognize the potential dangers and problems it poses. The erosion of personal agency is one of the most concerning consequences of an overemphasis on identity. By reclaiming personal agency and promoting a more nuanced understanding of identity, we can navigate the complexities of our diverse society while preserving individuality and autonomy.

Chapter 26: The Threat to Artistic Freedom in the Era of Identity Politics

In the era of identity politics, artistic freedom is under attack. The very essence of creativity and expression is being stifled by a dangerous ideology that seeks to control and dictate what can and cannot be said or depicted in art. This chapter explores the alarming threat that identity politics poses to artistic freedom, and why we must fight back against this encroachment on one of the most fundamental aspects of human civilization.

The Power of Art

Art has always been a powerful tool for self-expression, social commentary, and cultural exploration. It has the ability to challenge norms, provoke thought, and inspire change. Throughout history, artists have pushed boundaries, questioned authority, and given voice to the marginalized. Artistic freedom is essential for a thriving society, as it allows for the exploration of diverse perspectives and the fostering of empathy.

However, identity politics threatens to undermine this power by imposing strict limitations on what can be said or depicted in art. It seeks to control artistic expression by enforcing a narrow set of rules based on identity categories such as race, gender, sexuality, and religion. This not only stifles creativity but also perpetuates a culture of fear and self-censorship among artists.

The Danger of Censorship

Identity politics advocates argue that certain forms of art can be harmful or offensive to marginalized communities. While it is important to consider the impact of art on individuals and communities, censorship is not the solution. By censoring art that challenges or critiques identity-based ideologies, we risk erasing important conversations and silencing voices that need to be heard.

Censorship also undermines the very purpose of art, which is to provoke thought and engage in dialogue. Art has the power to challenge our preconceived notions, expose injustices, and spark conversations that lead to social change. By limiting artistic freedom, we limit our ability to address and confront the complex issues that plague our society.

The Loss of Nuance

Identity politics often reduces complex issues to simplistic narratives based on identity categories. This binary thinking fails to acknowledge the nuances and complexities of human experience. Artistic freedom allows for the exploration of these nuances, as artists can delve into the intricacies of human emotions, relationships, and societal structures.

When artistic expression is limited by identity politics, we lose the opportunity to engage with art that challenges our assumptions and expands our understanding of the world. We are left with a shallow representation of reality that fails to capture the depth and complexity of human existence.

The Threat to Creativity

Artistic freedom is essential for creativity to flourish. It allows artists to experiment, take risks, and push boundaries. By imposing rigid rules on what can and cannot be said or depicted in art, identity politics stifles this creativity and limits artistic innovation.

Artists should be free to explore controversial or uncomfortable topics without fear of retribution or censorship. It is through this exploration that new ideas are born, societal norms are challenged, and progress is made. Without artistic freedom, we risk stagnation and conformity in our cultural landscape.

Fighting Back

It is crucial that we fight back against the encroachment of identity politics on artistic freedom. We must defend the right of artists to express themselves without fear of censorship or retribution. This means challenging the notion that certain forms of art are inherently harmful or offensive.

We must also encourage and support diverse voices in the arts. By amplifying marginalized voices and providing platforms for underrepresented artists, we can ensure that a wide range of perspectives are represented in our cultural landscape.

Furthermore, we must engage in open and honest dialogue about the complexities of identity and representation in art. This means embracing nuance, challenging simplistic narratives, and fostering an environment where artists feel free to explore and express themselves without fear of backlash.

Artistic freedom is not a luxury; it is a fundamental human right. It is through art that we can challenge the status quo, imagine new possibilities, and create a more just and inclusive society. Let us not allow identity politics to strip us of this essential tool for social change.

Chapter 27: The Illusion of Social Justice in Identity Politics

Identity politics, the practice of organizing political movements around specific social identities, has gained significant traction in recent years. Proponents argue that it is a necessary tool for achieving social justice and equality. However, beneath the surface of this seemingly noble cause lies a dangerous ideology that threatens to undermine the very foundations of our society.

The Illusion of Social Justice

Perhaps the most insidious aspect of identity politics is its illusion of social justice. Proponents argue that by focusing on specific social identities, they are addressing historical injustices and working towards a more equitable society.

However, true social justice cannot be achieved by perpetuating divisions and hierarchies based on identity. It requires a holistic approach that recognizes the inherent worth and dignity of every individual, regardless of their social identities. By reducing individuals to mere representatives of their identity groups, identity politics fails to address the complex web of intersecting identities that make up each person's unique experience.

Furthermore, identity politics often overlooks the economic and class dimensions of inequality. By solely focusing on social identities, it neglects the structural factors that perpetuate poverty and marginalization. This narrow focus on identity alone risks creating a superficial form of justice that fails to address the root causes of inequality.

Conclusion

While the intentions behind identity politics may be noble, its implementation poses significant dangers to our society. The fragmentation of society, suppression of free speech, erosion of meritocracy, and illusion of social justice are all alarming consequences of this ideology.

If we truly want to achieve social justice and equality, we must move beyond the confines of identity politics. We must recognize the inherent worth and dignity of every individual, while also addressing the structural factors that perpetuate inequality. Only through a more inclusive and nuanced approach can we hope to build a society that is truly just and equitable for all.

Chapter 28: The Danger of Groupthink in Intersectional Activism

The Illusion of Intersectionality

Intersectionality is a key concept within identity politics that suggests individuals can experience multiple forms of oppression simultaneously due to their intersecting identities. While this idea may initially appear inclusive and empathetic, it ultimately leads to a dangerous form of uniformity of thought.

Intersectionality demands that individuals conform to a specific set of beliefs and opinions dictated by their group identities. Dissenting voices or alternative perspectives are dismissed as invalid or even oppressive. This stifling of intellectual diversity undermines critical thinking and hinders meaningful dialogue.

The Suppression of Individuality

Identity politics places an undue emphasis on group identity, effectively erasing the uniqueness and complexity of individuals. It reduces people to mere representatives of their social categories, denying them the agency to define themselves on their own terms.

This suppression of individuality is not only detrimental to personal growth and self-expression but also undermines the very essence of a free and democratic society. It restricts the ability of individuals to engage in open and honest conversations, as any deviation from the prescribed narrative is met with hostility and condemnation.

The Path to a Post-Identity Society

To overcome the dangers of identity politics, we must strive towards a post-identity society. This does not mean ignoring or erasing the existence of social categories but rather transcending their limitations and recognizing the inherent complexity and individuality of every person.

In a post-identity society, individuals are valued for their unique qualities and contributions rather than being reduced to mere representatives of their social groups. It is a society that embraces diversity of thought and encourages open dialogue, free from the constraints of a collective mindset and ideological conformity.

By rejecting the divisive and oppressive nature of identity politics, we can foster a society that celebrates individuality, promotes genuine equality, and upholds the principles of freedom and justice for all.

Chapter 29: The Weaponization of Language in Identity Politics

In the realm of identity politics, language has become a powerful weapon. Words and phrases that were once innocuous have been hijacked and redefined to serve a specific agenda. This weaponization of language is not only dangerous but also undermines the very foundations of open dialogue and intellectual discourse.

The Power of Language

Language is the primary tool through which we communicate our thoughts, ideas, and emotions. It is the medium through which we express ourselves and engage with others. When language is used as a weapon, it has the potential to manipulate, control, and silence.

Identity politics has taken advantage of this power by redefining words and phrases to fit its narrative. Terms like diversity, inclusion, and equality have been co-opted to mean something entirely different from their original intent. They are now used as weapons to shame, silence, and marginalize those who dare to question or disagree with the prevailing ideology.

The Weaponization of Diversity

The concept of diversity was originally meant to celebrate and embrace differences in race, ethnicity, gender, sexual orientation, and other characteristics. It was about creating an inclusive society where everyone had an equal opportunity to thrive.

However, in the world of identity politics, diversity has been weaponized to mean something entirely different. It has become a tool to enforce conformity of thought and suppress dissenting opinions. Those who do not conform to the prescribed narrative are labeled as privileged, oppressive, or even racist.

This weaponization of diversity has created a chilling effect on free speech and intellectual diversity. People are afraid to express their opinions or engage in open dialogue for fear of being labeled as bigots or haters. The result is an echo chamber where only one perspective is allowed, stifling the exchange of ideas and hindering intellectual growth.

The Weaponization of Inclusion

Inclusion, like diversity, was originally meant to promote a sense of belonging and acceptance for all individuals, regardless of their background or identity. It was about creating spaces where everyone felt valued and respected.

However, in the world of identity politics, inclusion has been weaponized to mean the exact opposite. It has become a tool to exclude and marginalize those who do not conform to the prevailing ideology. Those who hold different opinions or challenge the status quo are deemed unworthy of inclusion.

This weaponization of inclusion has created a culture of intolerance and exclusion. It has created a hierarchy of victimhood where certain groups are deemed more deserving of inclusion than others. This not only undermines the principles of equality but also perpetuates division and animosity among different groups.

The Weaponization of Equality

Equality, perhaps the most fundamental principle of a just society, has also fallen victim to the weaponization of language in identity politics. Originally meant to ensure equal rights and opportunities for all individuals, regardless of their background or identity, equality has been redefined to mean equal outcomes.

In the world of identity politics, equality is no longer about fairness or justice. It is about redistributing resources and privileges based on group identity rather than individual merit. This undermines the principles of individual liberty and personal responsibility, as it assumes that individuals are defined solely by their group identity.

This weaponization of equality has created a culture of entitlement and victimhood. It has fostered a mentality of grievance and resentment, where individuals are encouraged to see themselves as victims of systemic oppression rather than agents of their own destiny.

The Danger of Weaponized Language

The weaponization of language in identity politics is not only dangerous but also undermines the very foundations of open dialogue and intellectual discourse. It stifles free speech, silences dissenting voices, and creates a culture of fear and self-censorship.

When language is used as a weapon, it becomes a tool for manipulation and control. It allows those in power to dictate what can and cannot be said, what is acceptable and what is not. This not only hinders the exchange of ideas but also perpetuates division and animosity among different groups.

If we are to have meaningful conversations about the issues that affect us all, we must reclaim language from the clutches of identity politics. We must resist the weaponization of words and phrases and strive for open dialogue, intellectual diversity, and genuine understanding.

Only then can we truly address the challenges facing our society and work towards a more inclusive, equitable, and just future for all.

Chapter 30: The Fallacy of Collective Guilt in Identity Politics

Introduction

Identity politics has become a pervasive force in our society, infiltrating every aspect of our lives. It claims to fight for justice and equality, but in reality, it perpetuates a dangerous fallacy: the fallacy of collective guilt. This fallacy asserts that individuals are responsible for the actions and beliefs of their entire identity group, leading to division, resentment, and the erosion of individual rights. In this chapter, we will explore the dangers of collective guilt in identity politics and its detrimental effects on our society.

The Origins of Collective Guilt

Collective guilt is not a new concept; it has been used throughout history to justify discrimination, persecution, and even genocide. The idea that an entire group should be held responsible for the actions of a few is fundamentally flawed and morally bankrupt. Yet, identity politics has resurrected this dangerous notion under the guise of social justice.

The Fallacy of Collective Guilt

The fallacy of collective guilt rests on the assumption that individuals are defined solely by their identity group. It ignores the vast diversity within any given group and reduces individuals to mere representatives of their collective. This reductionist thinking not only erases individual agency but also perpetuates stereotypes and prejudices.

Furthermore, collective guilt assumes that all members of an identity group share the same beliefs and values. This generalization is not only inaccurate but also deeply unfair. It denies individuals the right to think independently and holds them accountable for actions they may vehemently oppose.

The Erosion of Individual Rights

Identity politics, with its emphasis on collective guilt, poses a significant threat to individual rights. When individuals are held responsible for the actions of their identity group, their freedom of thought and expression are stifled. Dissenting opinions are silenced, and conformity becomes the norm.

Moreover, the erosion of individual rights extends beyond freedom of thought. In the pursuit of social justice, identity politics often advocates for policies that prioritize group rights over individual rights. This leads to a dangerous imbalance where the rights of some are sacrificed for the perceived benefit of others.

The Danger of Resentment and Division

Collective guilt breeds resentment and division among different identity groups. When individuals are constantly reminded of their supposed complicity in historical injustices, it creates an atmosphere of hostility and animosity. Instead of fostering understanding and empathy, identity politics perpetuates a cycle of blame and victimhood.

Furthermore, collective guilt undermines the possibility of genuine dialogue and reconciliation. It discourages individuals from engaging in meaningful conversations about complex issues, as any dissenting opinion is seen as an attack on the entire group. This further entrenches divisions and prevents progress towards true equality.

Conclusion

The fallacy of collective guilt in identity politics is a dangerous ideology that threatens our society's core values. It erodes individual rights, perpetuates division and resentment, and stifles meaningful dialogue. To build a truly just and inclusive society, we must reject the notion that individuals should be held responsible for the actions and beliefs of their entire identity group. Only by recognizing the inherent worth and agency of each individual can we move towards a more equitable future.

Chapter 31: The Illusion of Moral Superiority in Identity Politics

The Dangers of Moral Certainty

One of the most alarming aspects of identity politics is the illusion of moral certainty it creates. Those who subscribe to this ideology believe that they possess an inherent moral superiority simply by virtue of their identity. They see themselves as righteous warriors fighting against an oppressive system.

This sense of moral certainty leads to a dangerous lack of self-reflection and critical thinking. When one believes they are on the side of righteousness, they become blind to their own flaws and biases. They dismiss any dissenting opinions as ignorant or bigoted, refusing to engage in meaningful dialogue.

Furthermore, the illusion of moral superiority in identity politics fosters a culture of victimhood. Individuals are encouraged to see themselves as perpetual victims, constantly oppressed by an unjust society. This victim mentality not only perpetuates a cycle of resentment and anger but also undermines personal agency and responsibility.

The Suppression of Individuality

Identity politics places such a strong emphasis on group identities that it often suppresses individuality. It reduces complex individuals to mere representatives of their respective groups, erasing their unique experiences, perspectives, and aspirations.

This suppression of individuality is detrimental to personal growth and intellectual development. It discourages individuals from exploring their own identities beyond the confines of their assigned group. It stifles creativity, critical thinking, and the pursuit of truth.

Breaking Free from the Illusion

It is crucial that we recognize the dangers of the illusion of moral superiority in identity politics. We must strive for a society that values individuality, critical thinking, and open dialogue. We must reject the reductionist approach of identity politics and embrace a more nuanced understanding of human experience.

By breaking free from the illusion of moral superiority, we can foster a culture that celebrates diversity of thought and encourages personal growth. We can create a society where individuals are judged not by the color of their skin or their gender but by the content of their character.

Let us not be blinded by the allure of moral certainty. Let us instead embrace the complexities of our shared humanity and work towards a future where true equality and justice can flourish.

Chapter 32: The Erosion of Individual Privacy by Identity Politics

In the age of identity politics, the concept of individual privacy is under attack. What was once considered a fundamental right is now being eroded by the relentless pursuit of group identity. As society becomes increasingly obsessed with categorizing individuals based on their race, gender, sexuality, and other characteristics, the notion of personal privacy is being sacrificed at the altar of collective identity.

The movement towards identity politics has led to a culture of constant surveillance and scrutiny. Individuals are now expected to publicly declare their identities and align themselves with specific groups. This pressure to conform to predetermined categories leaves little room for personal exploration and self-discovery.

The Weaponization of Identity

Identity politics has also led to the weaponization of identity. In an attempt to gain power and influence, individuals and groups often use their identities as a shield against criticism or accountability.

This weaponization of identity further erodes individual privacy by creating an environment of fear and self-censorship. Individuals are hesitant to speak out or challenge prevailing narratives for fear of being labeled as bigoted or intolerant. The result is a chilling effect on free speech and a narrowing of the public discourse.

The Loss of Personal Autonomy

Perhaps the most concerning aspect of the erosion of individual privacy by identity politics is the loss of personal autonomy. When individuals are constantly defined by their group identities, they are denied the agency to define themselves.

Personal autonomy is a fundamental aspect of human dignity. It allows individuals to make choices about their own lives, free from external pressures or expectations. The erosion of individual privacy by identity politics threatens this autonomy, leaving individuals feeling trapped and powerless.

Conclusion

The erosion of individual privacy by identity politics is a dangerous trend that must be addressed. While the pursuit of social justice and equality is important, it should not come at the expense of personal autonomy and privacy.

It is crucial that we recognize the value of individual experiences and allow for the complexity and nuance of human identity. Only by embracing individual privacy can we truly create a society that respects and celebrates the diversity of human existence.

Chapter 33: The Danger of Double Standards in Intersectional Ideology

The Double Standards of Intersectionality

Perhaps one of the most alarming aspects of intersectional ideology is its blatant double standards. While claiming to fight against discrimination and prejudice, intersectionalists often engage in discriminatory practices themselves.

For example, intersectionality promotes the idea that certain groups should be given preferential treatment in order to rectify historical injustices. This approach ignores the principle of equal opportunity and instead advocates for unequal treatment based on group identity.

Furthermore, intersectionality often dismisses or downplays the experiences and struggles of individuals who do not fit neatly into its prescribed categories. This exclusionary approach undermines the very principles of inclusivity and diversity that intersectionality claims to champion.

The Path Forward

It is crucial that we critically examine the dangers and problems with intersectional ideology. While it may have started with good intentions, it has evolved into a divisive and oppressive force that undermines individuality, free speech, and equality.

We must reject the reductionist approach of defining individuals solely by their group identities and instead embrace a more nuanced understanding of human complexity. We must also defend the principles of free speech and intellectual diversity, allowing for open and respectful dialogue.

Ultimately, we must strive for a society that values the inherent worth and dignity of every individual, regardless of their group identities. Only then can we truly achieve equality and justice for all.

Chapter 34: The Suppression of Dissenting Voices by Cancel Culture Warriors

In the age of identity politics, dissenting voices are being silenced at an alarming rate. The rise of cancel culture has created an environment where individuals who dare to challenge the prevailing narrative are ostracized, vilified, and even stripped of their livelihoods. This suppression of dissenting voices is not only a threat to free speech but also to the very foundations of a democratic society.

The Rise of Cancel Culture

Cancel culture, a term used to describe the practice of publicly shaming and boycotting individuals for their perceived offensive or problematic views, has gained significant traction in recent years. What was once a tool for holding powerful figures accountable has now morphed into a weapon used by self-appointed moral guardians to silence anyone who deviates from their prescribed ideology.

The cancel culture warriors claim to be fighting for social justice and equality, but their methods are anything but just. Instead of engaging in open dialogue and debate, they resort to character assassination and personal attacks. They create an atmosphere of fear and intimidation, where individuals are afraid to express their opinions for fear of being labeled as bigots or racists.

The Silencing Effect

The silencing effect of cancel culture is far-reaching and insidious. It not only stifles individual expression but also hampers intellectual growth and progress. When dissenting voices are suppressed, we lose the opportunity to engage in meaningful dialogue and challenge our own beliefs.

Cancel culture creates an echo chamber where only one perspective is allowed to thrive. This leads to consensus thinking and the erosion of critical thinking skills. When individuals are afraid to voice their opinions, they become passive consumers of information, accepting whatever is presented to them without question.

The Destruction of Careers

One of the most devastating consequences of cancel culture is the destruction of careers. Individuals who find themselves on the wrong side of the prevailing narrative can lose their jobs, their reputations, and their livelihoods overnight.

The cancel culture warriors have weaponized social media, using it as a platform to launch targeted campaigns against individuals they deem as problematic. They dig through years of someone's online presence, searching for any hint of a controversial statement or opinion. Once found, they pounce, demanding that the person be fired or otherwise punished.

This ruthless targeting not only affects the individual in question but also sends a chilling message to others who may dare to speak out. It creates a climate of fear and self-censorship, where individuals are afraid to express their true thoughts and feelings for fear of retribution.

The Threat to Free Speech

Cancel culture poses a significant threat to free speech, one of the fundamental pillars of a democratic society. The ability to express oneself freely and openly is essential for the exchange of ideas and the pursuit of truth.

When cancel culture warriors silence dissenting voices, they undermine the very essence of free speech. They create an environment where certain topics become off-limits and certain opinions are deemed unacceptable. This stifles intellectual diversity and hampers our ability to address complex issues.

Preserving Democracy

In order to preserve democracy and protect free speech, we must push back against cancel culture. We must create spaces where open dialogue and debate are encouraged, where individuals feel safe to express their opinions without fear of retribution.

We must also hold cancel culture warriors accountable for their actions.

While it is important to call out harmful behavior, we must do so in a way that promotes understanding and growth, rather than perpetuating a cycle of hate and division.

Ultimately, the suppression of dissenting voices by cancel culture warriors is a dangerous trend that threatens the very fabric of our society. We must stand up against this culture of fear and intimidation and fight for the principles that underpin our democracy.

Chapter 35: The Illusion of Progress in Identity Politics

The Illusion of Progress in Identity Politics

In this chapter, we will explore the illusion of progress in identity politics and the potential dangers it poses to our collective well-being.

The Illusion of Progress

Despite its claims to promote social justice and equality, identity politics ultimately fails to deliver on its promises. While it may provide temporary relief for marginalized communities, it does little to address the root causes of inequality and injustice. In fact, by perpetuating division and victimhood, identity politics often exacerbates these problems.

True progress can only be achieved through a holistic approach that recognizes the complexity of human experience and fosters unity rather than division. It requires us to move beyond the limitations of identity politics and embrace a more inclusive vision of society that values individuality, personal responsibility, and collective action.

Conclusion

The illusion of progress in identity politics is a dangerous ideology that threatens to undermine the very fabric of our society. By fragmenting society, suppressing individuality, and perpetuating victimhood, identity politics hinders meaningful dialogue, stifles personal growth, and perpetuates division. It is only through a rejection of this ideology and a commitment to unity and solidarity that we can truly achieve social justice and equality.

Chapter 36: The Threat to Intellectual Diversity by Identity Politics

In recent years, a dangerous ideology has been gaining traction in our society, threatening the very foundations of intellectual diversity. This ideology, known as identity politics, seeks to categorize individuals based on their immutable characteristics such as race, gender, and sexual orientation. While it claims to promote equality and social justice, identity politics is actually undermining the principles of free thought and open dialogue that are essential for a thriving intellectual community.

The Suppression of Dissenting Voices

One of the most alarming consequences of identity politics is the suppression of dissenting voices. In an environment where individuals are judged solely based on their identity, any deviation from the prevailing narrative is met with hostility and condemnation. This stifles intellectual debate and discourages individuals from expressing their opinions freely.

Imagine a world where every discussion is reduced to a battle between competing identities. Instead of engaging with ideas on their merits, individuals are forced to align themselves with a particular group and defend its interests at all costs. This tribalistic mentality not only hinders the pursuit of truth but also perpetuates division and animosity among different groups.

The Erosion of Intellectual Rigor

Identity politics also undermines intellectual rigor by prioritizing personal experiences over objective analysis. According to this ideology, an individual's perspective is determined solely by their identity, rendering any attempt at reasoned argumentation irrelevant.

This erosion of intellectual rigor is particularly concerning in academic institutions, where the pursuit of knowledge should be guided by rigorous research and critical thinking. When scholars are encouraged to prioritize personal narratives over empirical evidence, the integrity of academic disciplines is compromised, and the pursuit of truth becomes secondary to the validation of individual experiences.

The Threat to Intellectual Diversity

Ultimately, identity politics poses a significant threat to intellectual diversity. By reducing individuals to their immutable characteristics, this ideology discourages the exploration of different ideas and perspectives. It creates an environment where conformity is rewarded and dissent is punished.

Intellectual diversity is essential for the advancement of knowledge and the development of innovative solutions to complex problems. It requires a commitment to open dialogue, critical thinking, and the free exchange of ideas. Identity politics undermines these principles by prioritizing group identities over individual thought.

If we allow identity politics to continue unchecked, we risk creating an intellectual echo chamber where only certain perspectives are deemed acceptable. This not only stifles creativity and innovation but also undermines our ability to address the pressing challenges facing our society.

Conclusion

The rise of identity politics poses a grave threat to intellectual diversity. By suppressing dissenting voices, eroding intellectual rigor, fostering pack mentality, and undermining individual agency, this ideology undermines the very foundations of a thriving intellectual community.

To preserve intellectual diversity, we must reject the divisive and narrow-minded ideology of identity politics. We must embrace open dialogue, critical thinking, and the free exchange of ideas. Only by doing so can we ensure that our society remains a bastion of intellectual curiosity and innovation.

Chapter 37: The Fallacy of Group Identity in Intersectional Theory

Introduction

This chapter aims to expose the fallacy of group identity in intersectional theory and highlight the dangers it poses to our society.

The Reduction of Complex Individuals

One of the fundamental flaws of intersectional theory is its reductionist approach to human beings. By emphasizing group identities above all else, this ideology ignores the rich complexity of individuals. It fails to recognize that each person is a unique combination of experiences, beliefs, and aspirations that cannot be neatly categorized into predefined groups.

Reducing individuals to their group identities not only oversimplifies their existence but also perpetuates stereotypes and prejudices. It fosters an environment where people are judged based on superficial characteristics rather than their individual merits and achievements.

The Suppression of Individual Agency

Intersectional theory also undermines the concept of individual agency. By placing undue emphasis on group identities, it suggests that individuals have little control over their own lives and destinies. It implies that one's fate is predetermined by factors such as race or gender, leaving no room for personal growth or self-determination.

This suppression of individual agency is not only disempowering but also detrimental to societal progress. It discourages individuals from taking responsibility for their actions and pursuing their goals. Instead, it promotes a victim mentality where people believe they are powerless to change their circumstances, leading to a stagnant and unproductive society.

The Creation of Divisions

Perhaps the most alarming consequence of intersectional theory is its tendency to create divisions within society. By pitting different groups against each other based on their identities, it fosters an us versus them mentality that undermines social cohesion and unity.

Rather than promoting understanding and empathy between different groups, intersectional theory exacerbates existing tensions and fuels identity-based conflicts. It perpetuates a cycle of resentment and animosity, hindering any meaningful progress towards equality and justice.

The Erosion of Individual Rights

Another concerning aspect of intersectional theory is its potential to erode individual rights. By prioritizing group identities over individual freedoms, it opens the door for censorship, discrimination, and the suppression of dissenting voices.

In the name of protecting marginalized groups, intersectional theory often advocates for policies that infringe upon the rights of individuals who do not conform to its prescribed narratives. This not only undermines the principles of free speech and expression but also stifles intellectual diversity and critical thinking.

The Illusion of Equality

Despite its claims to promote equality, intersectional theory ultimately falls short in achieving this goal. By fixating on group identities, it perpetuates a form of identity-based hierarchy where certain groups are deemed more oppressed or privileged than others.

This hierarchy not only fails to address the complexities of individual experiences but also undermines the pursuit of true equality. It replaces one form of discrimination with another, perpetuating a never-ending cycle of division and resentment.

Conclusion

Intersectional theory, with its emphasis on group identities, is a deeply flawed and dangerous ideology. It reduces individuals to simplistic categories, suppresses individual agency, creates divisions within society, erodes individual rights, and fails to achieve true equality. As we navigate the complexities of our diverse world, it is crucial to reject this fallacious ideology and embrace a more nuanced understanding of human beings that celebrates our shared humanity while respecting our individual differences.

Chapter 38: The Illusion of Empowerment in Identity Politics

The Dangers of Essentialism

One of the most insidious aspects of identity politics is its reliance on essentialism. Essentialism is the belief that certain characteristics are inherent and unchangeable, defining an individual's entire existence. By promoting essentialism, identity politics denies the possibility of personal growth and development.

When individuals are told that their identity is fixed and unchangeable, it limits their potential for growth and self-improvement. It creates a mindset where individuals are trapped within the confines of their identity, unable to transcend societal expectations or challenge their own beliefs. This stagnation not only hinders personal development but also stifles intellectual discourse and progress.

The Illusion of Empowerment

Identity politics claims to empower marginalized groups by giving them a platform to voice their experiences and demand change. However, this so-called empowerment is nothing more than an illusion. In reality, identity politics perpetuates a cycle of dependency and victimhood.

By defining individuals solely based on their identity, identity politics reinforces the notion that they are inherently disadvantaged and incapable of success without external intervention. This creates a self-fulfilling prophecy where individuals believe they need constant protection and support from the state or other institutions. Instead of empowering individuals to take control of their own lives, identity politics fosters a culture of dependency and entitlement.

The Divisiveness of Identity Politics

Perhaps the most dangerous aspect of identity politics is its divisive nature. By emphasizing differences rather than commonalities, identity politics fuels animosity and hostility among different groups. It creates an us versus them mentality that erodes social cohesion and undermines the very foundations of a harmonious society.

When individuals are encouraged to view themselves solely through the lens of their identity, it becomes difficult to find common ground or engage in meaningful dialogue. Instead of fostering understanding and empathy, identity politics breeds resentment and division. It perpetuates a culture of tribalism, where individuals are pitted against each other based on their immutable characteristics.

The Way Forward

It is crucial that we recognize the dangers of identity politics and work towards a more inclusive and unified society. We must reject the reductionist approach of identity politics and embrace the complexity and diversity of human nature. By focusing on shared values and common goals, we can bridge the divides created by identity politics and build a society that celebrates individuality while fostering unity.

We must also encourage personal responsibility and agency, empowering individuals to take control of their own lives and strive for success based on merit rather than identity. By promoting a culture of self-reliance and accountability, we can break free from the cycle of victimhood perpetuated by identity politics.

Conclusion

Identity politics is a dangerous ideology that threatens to undermine the very foundations of our society. It perpetuates essentialism, victimhood, and division, while offering nothing more than an illusion of empowerment. It is time for us to reject this toxic ideology and work towards a society that values individuality, personal responsibility, and unity.

Chapter 39: The Erosion of Rational Discourse by Identity Politics

The Weaponization of Identity

Perhaps the most dangerous aspect of identity politics is its potential for weaponization. By dividing society into competing identity groups, it creates a fertile ground for conflict and animosity. The constant emphasis on grievances and historical injustices fuels resentment and perpetuates a cycle of blame.

Identity politics encourages individuals to view themselves as part of an oppressed group, pitted against other groups who are seen as oppressors. This divisive narrative not only undermines social cohesion but also hampers efforts towards genuine equality and justice. It replaces nuanced discussions about complex issues with simplistic binaries, further polarizing society.

Preserving Rational Discourse

To preserve rational discourse and critical thinking, we must challenge the corrosive influence of identity politics. We must recognize that individuals are more than just their group identities and encourage the exploration of diverse perspectives. It is crucial to foster an environment where dissenting opinions are welcomed and intellectual curiosity is nurtured.

We must also reject the victimhood narrative and promote personal responsibility and agency. By empowering individuals to take control of their own lives, we can break free from the cycle of victimhood and foster a culture of resilience and self-empowerment.

Lastly, we must strive for unity rather than division. Instead of focusing on our differences, we should seek common ground and work towards shared goals. By transcending identity politics, we can build a society that values individuality, promotes empathy, and encourages rational discourse.

Conclusion

The erosion of rational discourse by identity politics poses a grave threat to our society. It undermines critical thinking, perpetuates division, and stifles meaningful dialogue. To combat this dangerous trend, we must reclaim the principles of individualism, reject victimhood narratives, and strive for unity. Only then can we hope to preserve the foundations of rational discourse and create a society that values diversity, empathy, and intellectual growth.

Chapter 40: The Threat to Freedom of Association by Identity Politics

Introduction

While the intentions behind identity politics may be rooted in a desire for equality and justice, the consequences of this ideology pose a grave threat to one of the fundamental pillars of a free society: freedom of association.

The Erosion of Individuality

Identity politics promotes the idea that an individual's worth is determined solely by their group identity. This reductionist view erodes the importance of individuality and personal agency. Instead of valuing people for their unique qualities and accomplishments, identity politics encourages individuals to see themselves primarily as representatives of their group.

This erosion of individuality is particularly dangerous when it comes to freedom of association. If individuals are primarily defined by their group identity, it becomes increasingly difficult for them to form associations based on shared values, interests, or beliefs that transcend those identities. Instead, people are pressured to associate only with those who share their specific group characteristics.

Coercive Social Pressure

Identity politics also exerts coercive social pressure on individuals to conform to the expectations and demands of their identity group. Those who deviate from the prescribed narrative or challenge the prevailing orthodoxy risk being labeled as traitors or sellouts.

This coercive social pressure further restricts freedom of association by discouraging individuals from associating with those who may hold different views or belong to different identity groups. It creates an environment where people feel compelled to surround themselves only with those who share their specific identity, reinforcing echo chambers and hindering meaningful dialogue.

The Danger of Segregation

Identity politics, if taken to its extreme, can lead to a dangerous form of segregation. When individuals are encouraged to associate primarily with those who share their specific identity characteristics, it becomes increasingly difficult for diverse communities to form and thrive.

Segregation based on identity not only undermines the principles of equality and inclusivity but also restricts the ability of individuals to freely associate with those who may offer different perspectives, experiences, and opportunities. It hampers social progress and perpetuates divisions within society.

Conclusion

The rise of identity politics poses a significant threat to freedom of association. By eroding individuality, fostering conformity, exerting coercive social pressure, suppressing dissenting voices, and promoting segregation, this ideology undermines the very fabric of a free society.

To preserve freedom of association, it is crucial to reject the divisive and restrictive nature of identity politics. Instead, we must embrace a society that values individuality, encourages open dialogue, respects diverse perspectives, and promotes associations based on shared values and interests rather than immutable characteristics.

Chapter 41: The Fallacy of Collective Responsibility in Intersectional Activism

The Problem with Collective Responsibility

Collective responsibility is the notion that individuals are responsible for the actions and behaviors of their entire social group. In the context of intersectional activism, this means that individuals are held accountable for the actions and behaviors of all those who share their social identities. This concept is deeply flawed and dangerous for several reasons.

1. Individual Autonomy

One of the fundamental principles of a just society is individual autonomy - the idea that individuals should be held accountable for their own actions and not those of others. By imposing collective responsibility, intersectional activists undermine this principle and deny individuals their agency. It is unfair to hold someone responsible for actions they did not commit or beliefs they do not hold simply because they share a social identity with others who do.

2. Oversimplification of Complex Issues

Intersectional activism often oversimplifies complex issues by reducing them to a single dimension - social identity. This reductionist approach fails to acknowledge the complexity and diversity within social groups. Not all individuals within a particular social group think or act in the same way. By attributing collective responsibility to an entire group, intersectional activists ignore the nuances and individual experiences that shape people's beliefs and actions.

3. Reinforcement of Stereotypes

Collective responsibility perpetuates stereotypes and reinforces harmful biases. When individuals are held responsible for the actions of their social group, it reinforces the idea that all members of that group are the same. This not only erases individual differences but also perpetuates harmful stereotypes that can lead to discrimination and prejudice.

4. Inequality and Injustice

The fallacy of collective responsibility in intersectional activism can lead to inequality and injustice. By holding individuals accountable for the actions of their social group, it creates a system where some individuals are unfairly burdened with guilt or blame simply because of their social identities. This undermines the principles of fairness and equality that intersectional activists claim to champion.

The Path to Division

Collective responsibility in intersectional activism has the potential to further divide our society. By attributing blame and responsibility to entire social groups, it fosters an us versus them mentality that pits different groups against each other. This not only hinders progress towards equality and justice but also perpetuates a cycle of resentment and animosity.

Rather than promoting understanding and empathy, collective responsibility reinforces tribalism and identity-based divisions. It undermines the possibility of finding common ground and working towards shared goals.

Conclusion

While intersectional activism may have started with good intentions, the fallacy of collective responsibility undermines its goals and principles. Holding individuals accountable for the actions of their social group is unfair, oversimplifies complex issues, reinforces stereotypes, perpetuates inequality and injustice, stifles dissenting voices, and fosters division.

If we truly want to create a more just and equal society, we must reject the fallacy of collective responsibility and embrace individual autonomy, nuance, empathy, and open dialogue. Only then can we move towards a society that values the dignity and worth of every individual, regardless of their social identities.

Chapter 42: The Danger of Moral Absolutism in Identity Politics

The Danger of Moral Absolutism in Identity Politics

The rise of moral absolutism within identity politics is particularly concerning, as it stifles free thought, promotes division, and undermines the principles of individuality and personal responsibility.

The Suppression of Free Thought

One of the most alarming consequences of moral absolutism in identity politics is the suppression of free thought. In an environment where certain ideas are deemed morally wrong simply because they do not align with a particular group's identity, individuals are discouraged from engaging in critical thinking and exploring alternative perspectives. This stifling of intellectual diversity not only hampers progress but also creates a belief silo where dissenting voices are silenced.

By labeling any disagreement as an attack on one's identity, identity politics creates a climate of fear and self-censorship. People become afraid to express their opinions openly, for fear of being labeled as bigots or oppressors. This suppression of free thought is antithetical to the principles upon which our society was built - the freedom to express oneself and engage in open dialogue.

The Promotion of Division

Identity politics, with its emphasis on group identities, inherently promotes division among people. By categorizing individuals into rigid identity groups based on race, gender, or other characteristics, it fosters an us versus them mentality that pits different groups against each other. This division not only hinders social cohesion but also perpetuates a cycle of animosity and resentment.

Furthermore, the moral absolutism within identity politics often leads to a zero-sum game mentality, where one group's gain is seen as another group's loss. This creates a toxic environment where individuals are encouraged to view their own identity as superior and others as inherently oppressive. Such an approach only serves to deepen societal divisions and hinder any meaningful progress towards equality and understanding.

The Undermining of Individuality and Personal Responsibility

Identity politics places an excessive emphasis on group identity, often at the expense of individuality and personal responsibility. By reducing individuals to mere representatives of their identity groups, it denies them agency and perpetuates a victimhood narrative. This not only undermines the principles of personal responsibility but also hampers individual growth and self-empowerment.

Moreover, the moral absolutism within identity politics discourages individuals from taking responsibility for their own actions. Instead of holding individuals accountable for their choices and behaviors, it attributes everything to systemic oppression or privilege. This absolves individuals of any personal responsibility and perpetuates a culture of victimhood, where success or failure is determined solely by one's group identity.

The Way Forward

To address the dangers posed by moral absolutism in identity politics, we must strive for a more nuanced and inclusive approach. It is crucial to recognize that individuals are complex beings with multifaceted identities that cannot be reduced to a single characteristic or group affiliation.

We must foster an environment that encourages open dialogue, critical thinking, and intellectual diversity. This means embracing the discomfort that comes with engaging with ideas that challenge our own beliefs and being willing to consider alternative perspectives.

Furthermore, we must shift the focus from group identities to individual experiences and aspirations. By empowering individuals to take ownership of their own lives and choices, we can foster a culture of personal responsibility and self-empowerment.

Conclusion

The moral absolutism within identity politics poses a significant threat to our society. It suppresses free thought, promotes division, and undermines individuality and personal responsibility. To overcome these dangers, we must reject the rigid categorization of individuals based on identity and instead embrace a more inclusive and nuanced approach that values open dialogue, intellectual diversity, and individual agency.

Chapter 43: The Threat to Academic Freedom by Identity Politics

In recent years, a dangerous ideology has been spreading like wildfire across college campuses and academic institutions. This ideology, known as identity politics, poses a significant threat to academic freedom and the pursuit of knowledge. Under the guise of promoting equality and social justice, identity politics has created an environment of fear and censorship, stifling intellectual diversity and critical thinking.

The Suppression of Dissenting Voices

One of the most alarming aspects of identity politics is its tendency to suppress dissenting voices. Those who dare to question or challenge the prevailing orthodoxy are often labeled as bigots or oppressors. This creates a chilling effect on free speech and intellectual inquiry.

Professors who hold unpopular views or engage in research that contradicts the prevailing narrative are at risk of being ostracized or even losing their jobs. This not only stifles academic freedom but also deprives students of exposure to diverse perspectives and ideas.

The Decline of Intellectual Diversity

Identity politics has led to a decline in intellectual diversity within academic institutions. The pressure to conform to a particular set of beliefs and values discourages open dialogue and critical thinking. As a result, students are denied the opportunity to engage in robust debates and challenge their own assumptions.

This lack of intellectual diversity undermines the very purpose of higher education, which is to expose students to a wide range of ideas and perspectives. Without exposure to diverse viewpoints, students are ill-equipped to navigate the complexities of the real world and make informed decisions.

The Erosion of Objective Truth

Identity politics also poses a threat to the concept of objective truth. In the world of identity politics, truth is seen as subjective and dependent on one's personal experiences and identities. This relativistic view undermines the pursuit of knowledge and rational inquiry.

When truth becomes a matter of personal perspective, it becomes impossible to have meaningful discussions or reach consensus on important issues. This erosion of objective truth not only hinders intellectual progress but also undermines the foundations of a democratic society.

The Danger of Mob Mentality

Identity politics fosters an environment of mob mentality, where conformity is valued over independent thought. In this opinion reinforcement zone, individuals are discouraged from questioning or challenging the prevailing narrative. Dissent is seen as a betrayal rather than an essential part of intellectual growth.

Mob mentality stifles creativity, innovation, and critical thinking. It creates an intellectual monoculture where only certain ideas are deemed acceptable, while others are dismissed without consideration. This narrow-mindedness is antithetical to the principles of academic freedom and the pursuit of knowledge.

The Way Forward

To protect academic freedom and the pursuit of knowledge, it is crucial to challenge the dominance of identity politics within academic institutions. This requires fostering an environment that values intellectual diversity, encourages open dialogue, and promotes critical thinking.

Professors and students must be free to explore controversial ideas, engage in rigorous debate, and challenge prevailing narratives without fear of retribution. Only by embracing intellectual diversity can we ensure that our universities remain vibrant centers of learning and innovation.

It is time to recognize the dangers of identity politics and reclaim the principles of academic freedom. The future of higher education depends on it.

Chapter 44: The Fallacy of Social Conformity in Identity Politics Movements

Introduction

Identity politics movements have gained significant traction in recent years, with individuals and groups rallying around their shared identities to fight for social justice and equality. While the intentions behind these movements may be noble, there is a dangerous fallacy that underlies the very foundation of identity politics: social conformity. This chapter aims to explore the fallacy of social conformity within identity politics movements and shed light on the potential dangers and problems that arise as a result.

The Illusion of Homogeneity

One of the fundamental flaws of identity politics is the assumption that individuals within a particular identity group share the same beliefs, values, and experiences. This illusion of homogeneity leads to a dangerous oversimplification of complex issues and stifles meaningful dialogue. By reducing individuals to mere representatives of their identity group, identity politics fails to acknowledge the diversity and individuality within each group.

This oversimplification not only undermines the complexity of human experiences but also perpetuates stereotypes and reinforces divisions between different identity groups. It creates an us versus them mentality, where any dissenting opinions or alternative perspectives are dismissed as betrayals or acts of oppression. In this way, social conformity becomes a self-perpetuating cycle within identity politics movements.

The Suppression of Individuality

Identity politics movements often demand strict adherence to a particular set of beliefs and values deemed appropriate for a specific identity group. This demand for conformity suppresses individuality and discourages critical thinking. Dissenting voices within these movements are often silenced or ostracized, leading to a chilling effect on free speech.

The suppression of individuality not only stifles intellectual growth but also hinders the ability to address the complexities of social issues. By discouraging dissent and alternative viewpoints, identity politics movements limit their own capacity for self-reflection and growth. This lack of internal critique can lead to a dangerous ideological cocoon, where ideas go unchallenged and extremism flourishes.

The Danger of Essentialism

Identity politics often relies on essentialist notions of identity, reducing individuals to a set of fixed characteristics based on their race, gender, sexuality, or other identity markers. This essentialism ignores the fluidity and complexity of human experiences and perpetuates harmful stereotypes.

Essentialism not only erases the diversity within identity groups but also reinforces harmful notions of superiority or victimhood. It creates a hierarchy of oppression, where individuals are valued or dismissed based on their perceived level of victimhood. This reductionist approach fails to acknowledge the intersectionality of identities and the unique challenges faced by individuals who may belong to multiple marginalized groups.

The Erosion of Empathy

Identity politics movements often prioritize the experiences and perspectives of certain identity groups over others. While this prioritization may be well-intentioned, it can lead to a lack of empathy towards individuals who do not fit neatly into predefined categories.

By focusing solely on one's own identity group, individuals within identity politics movements may fail to recognize the struggles faced by those outside their immediate sphere. This lack of empathy can further polarize society and hinder efforts towards genuine understanding and collaboration.

The Threat to Democracy

Identity politics movements pose a significant threat to democracy by undermining the principles of individual liberty and equality. By prioritizing group identities over individual rights, these movements risk creating a society where individuals are judged solely based on their group affiliations rather than their character or actions.

Furthermore, the fallacy of consensus thought within identity politics can lead to the suppression of dissenting voices and the erosion of democratic values such as free speech and open dialogue. In a healthy democracy, diverse perspectives should be encouraged and debated, rather than silenced or dismissed.

Conclusion

While identity politics movements may have emerged as a response to genuine social injustices, it is crucial to recognize and address the fallacy of social conformity that underlies these movements. By acknowledging the diversity and complexity within identity groups, fostering individuality and critical thinking, rejecting essentialism, promoting empathy, and upholding democratic values, we can move towards a more inclusive and equitable society.

Chapter 45: The Danger of Moral Relativism in Intersectional Theory

The Danger of Moral Relativism in Intersectional Theory

In recent years, a new ideology has emerged that threatens to undermine the very fabric of our society. This ideology, known as intersectional theory, promotes the idea that individuals should be defined by their multiple intersecting identities, such as race, gender, and sexual orientation. While on the surface this may seem like a noble pursuit for equality and justice, it is important to recognize the dangers that lie beneath the surface.

The Rejection of Objective Truth

One of the most alarming aspects of intersectional theory is its rejection of objective truth. According to this ideology, truth is not something that exists independently of our subjective experiences, but rather something that is constructed through our individual perspectives. This leads to a dangerous form of moral relativism, where there are no universal standards by which we can judge right from wrong.

Without a shared understanding of what is morally right and wrong, society becomes fragmented and chaotic. Intersectional theory encourages individuals to prioritize their own personal experiences over any objective truth, leading to a society where everyone's truth is equally valid. This not only undermines the concept of justice but also erodes the very foundations of our legal system.

The Erosion of Individual Responsibility

Intersectional theory also undermines the concept of individual responsibility. By placing the blame for societal inequalities solely on systems of power and privilege, it absolves individuals of any personal responsibility for their own actions and choices.

While it is true that systems of power can perpetuate inequality, it is also important to recognize that individuals have agency and the ability to make choices that can improve their own lives. Intersectional theory, however, denies this agency and instead promotes a victim mentality where individuals are seen as passive recipients of oppression.

The Division of Society

Perhaps the most dangerous consequence of intersectional theory is its tendency to divide society into competing identity groups. By emphasizing differences rather than commonalities, intersectional theory fosters a sense of tribalism and animosity between different groups.

This division not only hinders social cohesion but also prevents us from working together to address the real issues that affect us all. Instead of focusing on shared goals and values, intersectional theory encourages us to view each other as adversaries in a never-ending battle for power and recognition.

A Call for Rationality

In order to address the dangers posed by intersectional theory, we must reject the notion that truth is subjective and embrace the idea that there are objective standards by which we can judge right from wrong. We must also defend the principles of free speech and individual responsibility, recognizing that these are essential for a healthy and functioning society.

Furthermore, we must strive to bridge the divides that intersectional theory has created and find common ground with those who hold different perspectives. Only through open and respectful dialogue can we hope to overcome the challenges that face us and build a society that is truly just and equitable for all.

Chapter 46: The Illusion of Social Justice Achieved through Identity Politics

The Illusion of Social Justice Achieved through Identity Politics

The Illusion of Social Justice

One of the most insidious aspects of identity politics is its claim to fight for social justice. While it may appear to champion the cause of equality, it actually perpetuates a form of inequality by prioritizing certain groups over others. By focusing solely on group identity, identity politics ignores the unique struggles faced by individuals within those groups.

True social justice can only be achieved by recognizing the inherent worth and dignity of every individual, regardless of their group identity. It requires us to move beyond the narrow confines of identity politics and embrace a more inclusive and holistic approach to equality.

Rejecting Identity Politics

It is time for us to reject the divisive ideology of identity politics and reclaim our shared humanity. We must recognize that true progress can only be achieved through unity, understanding, and empathy.

Instead of focusing on what divides us, we should strive to find common ground and work towards solutions that benefit all members of society. We must reject the notion that one's worth is determined solely by their group identity and instead judge individuals based on their character, actions, and ideas.

By rejecting identity politics, we can create a society that values individuality, fosters meaningful dialogue, and promotes true social justice. It is only through this rejection that we can hope to build a better future for ourselves and future generations.

Chapter 47: The Threat to Individual Liberty by Equity Policies

This chapter aims to shed light on the dangers and problems associated with this ideology, and the urgent need to address them.

Discrimination Disguised as Equity

Equity policies, often championed by proponents of identity politics, claim to address historical inequalities by redistributing resources and opportunities based on group membership. However, these policies often result in reverse discrimination against individuals who do not fit into designated victim or privileged groups. Meritocracy is sacrificed in favor of arbitrary quotas, leading to the exclusion of qualified individuals solely based on their identity. This not only undermines individual liberty but also hampers societal progress by stifling innovation and rewarding mediocrity.

The Danger of Identity Silos

Identity politics has inadvertently created silos within society, where individuals primarily interact with others who share their identity. This leads to belief bubbles, where differing perspectives are rarely encountered or seriously considered. As a result, empathy and understanding between different groups diminish, further polarizing society and hindering efforts to find common ground.

The Path Forward: Individualism and Equality

To safeguard individual liberty and promote true equality, it is crucial to reject the divisive ideology of identity politics. Instead, we must embrace a philosophy that values individualism while striving for equal opportunities for all. By focusing on the content of one's character rather than their immutable characteristics, we can foster a society that respects individual autonomy, encourages intellectual diversity, and promotes genuine equality.

Conclusion

Identity politics poses a significant threat to individual liberty. Its emphasis on group identity over individual autonomy, reverse discrimination disguised as equity, suppression of free speech and intellectual diversity, and the creation of identity silos all undermine the principles upon which our society is built. It is imperative that we recognize these dangers and work towards a more inclusive and individualistic approach that upholds the values of liberty, justice, and equality for all.

Chapter 48: The Fallacy of Collective Guilt and Innocence in Intersectional Activism

Introduction

In this chapter, we will explore the dangers and problems with this ideology, and why it is imperative that we reject it.

The Fallacy of Collective Guilt

One of the central tenets of intersectional activism is the concept of collective guilt. According to this ideology, individuals are not solely responsible for their own actions but are instead implicated in the historical injustices committed by their ancestors or members of their racial or ethnic group. This fallacious reasoning ignores the fundamental principle of individual agency and holds individuals accountable for crimes they did not commit.

By assigning collective guilt based on group identity, intersectional activists perpetuate a cycle of blame and resentment that hinders progress towards true equality. Instead of encouraging dialogue and understanding between different groups, this ideology fosters division and animosity. It creates an us versus them mentality that undermines the possibility of genuine reconciliation and cooperation.

The Danger of Collective Innocence

While intersectional activism promotes collective guilt for some groups, it simultaneously bestows collective innocence upon others. This double standard is deeply problematic as it perpetuates a distorted view of history and absolves individuals from taking responsibility for their own actions.

By assigning collective innocence based on group identity, intersectional activists create a hierarchy of victimhood where certain groups are deemed inherently virtuous and blameless. This not only undermines the concept of personal agency but also denies individuals within these groups the opportunity to grow and learn from their own mistakes. It fosters a culture of victimhood and entitlement, where individuals are shielded from criticism or accountability.

The Erosion of Individuality

One of the most insidious consequences of intersectional activism is the erosion of individuality. By reducing individuals to mere representatives of their group identity, this ideology denies the complexity and diversity of human experience. It disregards the unique circumstances, choices, and aspirations that shape each person's life.

When we prioritize group identity over individuality, we risk stifling dissenting voices and discouraging independent thought. This homogenization of perspectives undermines the very essence of a free and democratic society, where individuals should be encouraged to express their own opinions and challenge prevailing narratives.

The Illusion of Social Justice

Intersectional activism claims to champion social justice, but in reality, it perpetuates injustice by promoting a system that judges individuals based on immutable characteristics rather than their actions or character. This ideology fails to recognize that true justice can only be achieved through the fair treatment of individuals as unique beings with their own agency.

By focusing on collective guilt and innocence, intersectional activism distracts from the real issues at hand – poverty, inequality, discrimination – that affect individuals regardless of their group identity. It perpetuates a divisive narrative that pits groups against each other instead of fostering solidarity and cooperation.

Conclusion

The fallacy of collective guilt and innocence in intersectional activism is a dangerous ideology that threatens the very fabric of our society. By assigning blame or absolution based on group identity, this ideology undermines individual agency, erodes personal responsibility, and perpetuates division. It is imperative that we reject this ideology and instead embrace a society that values individuality, personal accountability, and genuine social justice.

Chapter 49: The Weaponization of Language to Silence Dissent in Identity Politics

Introduction

One of the most insidious tactics employed by identity politics is the weaponization of language. By manipulating words and redefining their meanings, proponents of this ideology have effectively created a minefield where any misstep can lead to public shaming, career destruction, and social isolation.

The Power of Language

Language is a powerful tool that shapes our thoughts, beliefs, and actions. It allows us to communicate complex ideas, express our emotions, and engage in meaningful dialogue. However, when language is weaponized, it becomes a potent instrument of control and manipulation.

Identity politics activists have mastered the art of linguistic manipulation. They have created an ever-expanding lexicon of terms that are used to label and categorize individuals based on their perceived identities. These labels are not meant to foster understanding or empathy but rather to divide and conquer.

The Tyranny of Political Correctness

One of the most alarming consequences of the weaponization of language is the rise of political correctness. Under the guise of promoting inclusivity and sensitivity, identity politics activists have imposed a strict set of rules governing what can and cannot be said.

This new form of censorship stifles open debate and intellectual inquiry. It creates an environment where individuals are afraid to express their opinions for fear of being labeled as bigots or oppressors. Dissent is not tolerated, and any deviation from the prescribed narrative is met with swift and severe consequences.

The Weaponization of Labels

Identity politics activists have weaponized labels to silence dissenting voices. Terms like racist, sexist, and homophobic are thrown around with reckless abandon, often without any basis in reality. These labels are used not to engage in meaningful dialogue but to shut down the conversation entirely.

By labeling someone as a bigot, identity politics activists effectively delegitimize their opinions and invalidate their experiences. This tactic is particularly effective because it preys on our innate desire to be seen as good and moral individuals. No one wants to be labeled as a racist or a sexist, so many people choose to self-censor rather than risk being ostracized.

The Destruction of Nuance

Another consequence of the weaponization of language is the destruction of nuance. Identity politics activists have created a binary worldview where individuals are either oppressors or victims, with no room for complexity or individuality.

This black-and-white thinking leaves no space for disagreement or debate. It reduces complex issues to simplistic slogans and soundbites, preventing us from engaging in meaningful conversations about the challenges we face as a society.

The Silencing of Dissent

Perhaps the most troubling aspect of the weaponization of language is its chilling effect on free speech. In an environment where any deviation from the prescribed narrative is met with public shaming and career destruction, individuals are forced to self-censor.

This silencing of dissent stifles innovation, creativity, and progress. It prevents us from challenging prevailing ideas and exploring new perspectives. It creates an echo chamber where only one viewpoint is allowed, leading to intellectual stagnation and the erosion of democratic values.

Conclusion

The weaponization of language in identity politics is a dangerous trend that threatens the very foundations of our society. By manipulating words and redefining their meanings, proponents of this ideology have effectively silenced dissent and stifled free speech.

We must recognize the dangers of this tactic and reclaim the power of language. We must foster an environment where open debate and intellectual inquiry are encouraged, and where individuals are free to express their opinions without fear of retribution.

Only by challenging the weaponization of language can we hope to restore civility, empathy, and understanding in our society.

Chapter 50: The Suppression of Intellectual Diversity by Cancel Culture Zealots

Introduction

In recent years, a dangerous trend has emerged within our society - the rise of cancel culture zealots who seek to suppress intellectual diversity and stifle free expression. Under the guise of promoting social justice and equality, these self-appointed guardians of morality have created an environment of fear and censorship, where any dissenting opinion is met with swift and severe consequences. This chapter aims to shed light on the dangers posed by these ideologues and the impact they have on our intellectual landscape.

The Origins of Cancel Culture

Cancel culture, also known as call-out culture, can be traced back to the early days of social media. With the advent of platforms like Twitter and Facebook, individuals gained unprecedented power to publicly shame and ostracize those who held differing views. What started as a means to hold public figures accountable for their actions quickly spiraled into a weapon used by ideologues to silence anyone who dared to challenge their beliefs.

The proponents of cancel culture argue that it is necessary to create a safe space for marginalized communities by silencing dissenting voices. They claim that certain ideas are inherently harmful and should not be given a platform. However, this approach undermines the very essence of intellectual diversity - the idea that different perspectives are essential for the growth and development of society.

The Threat to Intellectual Diversity

One of the most significant dangers posed by cancel culture is its suppression of intellectual diversity. By creating an environment where certain ideas are deemed off-limits, cancel culture zealots limit our ability to engage in meaningful dialogue and debate. This stifling of diverse perspectives hampers our collective progress as a society.

In the pursuit of social justice, cancel culture zealots have created a narrow framework within which discussions can take place. Any deviation from this framework is met with accusations of bigotry, racism, or sexism. This not only discourages individuals from expressing their opinions but also prevents the exploration of alternative solutions to complex problems.

The Fear Factor

Cancel culture thrives on fear. The fear of being publicly shamed, losing one's job, or being ostracized from social circles is a powerful deterrent for individuals who may hold unpopular opinions. This fear leads to self-censorship, where individuals refrain from expressing their thoughts and ideas out of concern for the consequences.

The chilling effect of cancel culture is particularly detrimental to academia and intellectual discourse. Universities, once bastions of free thought and open debate, have become breeding grounds for conformity and ideological orthodoxy. Professors and students alike are hesitant to challenge prevailing narratives for fear of retribution.

The Illusion of Virtue

Cancel culture zealots often present themselves as virtuous crusaders fighting for justice and equality. They believe that by silencing dissenting voices, they are creating a more inclusive society. However, this illusion of virtue masks the true nature of their actions - the suppression of intellectual diversity and the erosion of free expression.

True progress can only be achieved through open dialogue and the exchange of ideas. By shutting down conversations and labeling opposing viewpoints as inherently harmful, cancel culture zealots hinder our ability to find common ground and work towards meaningful change.

The Path Forward

To combat the dangers posed by cancel culture, we must reclaim the value of intellectual diversity and free expression. It is essential to create spaces where individuals feel safe to express their opinions without fear of retribution. This requires fostering a culture of open-mindedness, empathy, and respect for differing viewpoints.

Furthermore, it is crucial to challenge the notion that certain ideas are inherently harmful and should be silenced. Instead of shutting down conversations, we should encourage robust debate and critical thinking. By engaging with opposing viewpoints, we can strengthen our own arguments and develop a more nuanced understanding of complex issues.

Conclusion

The suppression of intellectual diversity by cancel culture zealots poses a significant threat to our society. By creating an environment of fear and censorship, these ideologues hinder our ability to engage in meaningful dialogue and stifle the progress of our collective intellect. It is imperative that we resist this dangerous trend and reclaim the value of free expression and intellectual diversity.

Chapter 51: The Rise of Identity Politics in Media and Entertainment

The Influence of Media and Entertainment

Media and entertainment play a significant role in shaping public opinion and influencing cultural norms. Unfortunately, many outlets have embraced identity politics as a means to attract audiences and promote a particular agenda.

Television shows, movies, and even news programs often prioritize representation over storytelling and quality. Characters are now created and cast based on their identity rather than their talent or suitability for a role. This tokenism reduces complex individuals to mere stereotypes, perpetuating harmful generalizations and reinforcing divisions between groups.

Furthermore, the media's obsession with identity politics has led to a stifling of free expression and open dialogue. Any dissenting opinion or nuanced discussion is labeled as offensive or oppressive, effectively silencing those who dare to question the prevailing narrative. This creates an echo chamber where only certain perspectives are allowed, hindering our ability to engage in meaningful conversations and find common ground.

The Dangers of Identity Politics in Media

The rise of identity politics in media and entertainment poses several dangers to our society:

1. Division: Identity politics perpetuates a divisive us versus them mentality, pitting different groups against each other. This not only hinders social cohesion but also prevents us from addressing the real issues that affect all members of society.

2. Stereotyping: By reducing individuals to their identities, media outlets reinforce harmful stereotypes that do not accurately reflect the complexity of human experiences. This leads to further marginalization and discrimination.

3. Suppression of Free Speech: The dominance of identity politics in media has created an environment where dissenting opinions are silenced and open dialogue is discouraged. This stifles intellectual growth and prevents us from challenging prevailing ideas.

4. Loss of Individuality: Identity politics undermines the importance of personal responsibility and individual achievement by placing undue emphasis on group identity. This discourages individuals from taking ownership of their actions and pursuing their own goals.

5. Polarization: The focus on identity politics in media and entertainment has led to an increasingly polarized society. People are more likely to view those with different identities as enemies rather than fellow citizens, making it difficult to find common ground and work towards shared goals.

The Way Forward

It is crucial that we recognize the dangers of identity politics in media and entertainment and take steps to counteract its influence. We must prioritize storytelling, quality, and open dialogue over tokenism and ideological agendas.

Media outlets should strive to represent a diverse range of perspectives and experiences without reducing individuals to stereotypes. They should promote nuanced discussions that allow for dissenting opinions and encourage critical thinking.

As consumers of media, we must also be vigilant in our consumption. We should seek out diverse voices and perspectives, challenge prevailing narratives, and engage in respectful dialogue with those who hold different views.

By rejecting the divisive ideology of identity politics in media and entertainment, we can foster a more inclusive society that values individuality, free expression, and the pursuit of common goals. It is only through unity and understanding that we can overcome the challenges we face as a society.

Chapter 52: The Threat to Freedom of Thought by Ideological Indoctrination

In an environment dominated by identity politics, dissenting opinions are often met with hostility and accusations of bigotry. This creates a chilling effect on free speech, as individuals fear the social and professional consequences of expressing unpopular views. The result is a society in which conformity is valued over independent thought, and intellectual curiosity is stifled.

The Suppression of Dissenting Voices

Identity politics also poses a threat to freedom of thought by actively suppressing dissenting voices. Those who dare to question the prevailing orthodoxy are often labeled as heretics and subjected to public shaming and ostracism. This not only silences individuals who hold unpopular opinions but also discourages others from engaging in critical thinking.

The suppression of dissenting voices is particularly prevalent in educational institutions, where students are exposed to a narrow range of perspectives and discouraged from questioning the prevailing narrative. This indoctrination not only undermines the pursuit of knowledge but also deprives students of the opportunity to develop their own independent thoughts and ideas.

The Threat to Academic Freedom

Perhaps one of the most alarming aspects of identity politics is its assault on academic freedom. In an era where universities were once bastions of free thought and intellectual inquiry, they have now become breeding grounds for ideological conformity.

Professors who deviate from the prevailing orthodoxy risk losing their jobs or facing professional repercussions. Students who express dissenting opinions are often subjected to disciplinary action or social ostracism. This climate of fear and intimidation stifles intellectual debate and undermines the very purpose of higher education – to foster critical thinking and independent thought.

Preserving Freedom of Thought

In order to preserve our freedom of thought, we must resist the encroachment of identity politics into our society. We must reject the reductionist view of human beings as mere representatives of their respective groups and instead embrace the complexity and diversity of the human experience.

We must also encourage intellectual diversity and create spaces where individuals feel safe to express their opinions, even if they are unpopular or controversial. This means fostering an environment of open dialogue and respectful debate, where ideas are evaluated on their merits rather than the identity of the person expressing them.

Finally, we must reaffirm our commitment to academic freedom and ensure that our educational institutions remain places of intellectual inquiry and free thought. This requires protecting the rights of professors and students to express dissenting opinions without fear of retribution.

Conclusion

The rise of identity politics poses a grave threat to our freedom of thought. By fostering a herd mentality, suppressing dissenting voices, and undermining academic freedom, this ideology threatens to stifle intellectual diversity and hinder the progress of our society. It is up to us to resist this dangerous trend and preserve the fundamental right to independent thought.

Chapter 53: The Fallacy of Group Identity as the Sole Determinant in Intersectional Theory

The Dangers of Group Identity

In recent years, there has been a growing trend towards embracing identity politics and intersectional theory. While the intention behind these movements may be noble, it is crucial to critically examine the fallacy of group identity as the sole determinant in intersectional theory. This chapter aims to shed light on the dangers and problems associated with this ideology.

1. Oversimplification of Complex Identities

One of the fundamental flaws of identity politics is its tendency to oversimplify complex identities. Intersectionality asserts that an individual's experiences and privileges are solely determined by their group identities, such as race, gender, or sexual orientation. This reductionist approach fails to acknowledge the multifaceted nature of human beings and ignores the unique experiences and perspectives that individuals bring to the table.

By reducing individuals to mere representatives of their group identities, intersectional theory undermines the importance of personal agency and individuality. It perpetuates a divisive narrative that pits groups against each other, fostering an us versus them mentality that hinders meaningful dialogue and collaboration.

2. The Tyranny of Victimhood

Identity politics often promotes a culture of victimhood, where individuals are encouraged to view themselves primarily as victims of systemic oppression. While it is essential to acknowledge and address systemic inequalities, an overemphasis on victimhood can lead to a dangerous cycle of blame and resentment.

When individuals are constantly told that their group identity determines their worth and experiences, it can create a sense of helplessness and dependency on external forces for change. This victim mentality undermines personal responsibility and agency, hindering individuals from taking proactive steps towards empowerment and self-improvement.

3. Divisiveness and Polarization

Identity politics has the potential to create deep divisions within society. By emphasizing group identities as the primary lens through which individuals should be understood, it fosters an us versus them mentality that perpetuates animosity and polarization.

When individuals are encouraged to view themselves primarily as members of a particular group, it becomes increasingly challenging to find common ground and build bridges between different communities. This divisiveness hampers progress towards a more inclusive and harmonious society, as it reinforces stereotypes, prejudices, and discrimination.

4. Suppression of Individuality

Identity politics often overlooks the importance of individuality and personal agency. By placing undue emphasis on group identities, it fails to recognize the unique experiences, perspectives, and aspirations that make each person distinct.

When individuals are reduced to representatives of their group identities, their individual achievements, talents, and contributions are overshadowed. This suppression of individuality not only undermines personal growth but also stifles creativity, innovation, and diversity of thought.

5. Inherent Contradictions

Intersectional theory often falls victim to inherent contradictions. While it aims to address systemic inequalities by highlighting the experiences of marginalized groups, it can inadvertently perpetuate new forms of discrimination and exclusion.

For example, intersectionality suggests that certain groups are inherently privileged or oppressed based on their group identities. However, this oversimplification fails to account for the vast diversity within these groups and ignores the complex interplay of various factors that shape an individual's experiences.

Furthermore, intersectionality often prioritizes certain group identities over others, creating a hierarchy of victimhood that can lead to the marginalization of individuals who do not fit neatly into predefined categories.

Conclusion

While identity politics and intersectional theory may have emerged as a response to systemic inequalities, it is crucial to critically examine their limitations and potential dangers. The fallacy of group identity as the sole determinant in intersectional theory oversimplifies complex identities, fosters a culture of victimhood, promotes divisiveness and polarization, suppresses individuality, and perpetuates inherent contradictions.

To build a more inclusive and equitable society, we must move beyond the confines of identity politics and embrace a more nuanced understanding of human experiences that recognizes the importance of both group identities and individual agency.

Chapter 54: The Danger of Ideological Echo Chambers in Academic Institutions

In recent years, academic institutions have become breeding grounds for a dangerous phenomenon known as identity politics. This ideology, which focuses on the primacy of individual identity and the power dynamics associated with it, has infiltrated every aspect of academia, from classrooms to research papers. While it may seem harmless at first glance, the rise of identity politics poses a significant threat to intellectual diversity, critical thinking, and the pursuit of knowledge.

The Suppression of Dissenting Voices

One of the most alarming consequences of identity politics is the suppression of dissenting voices. In an ideological echo chamber, where only one perspective is allowed to thrive, any deviation from the accepted narrative is met with hostility and ostracization. This stifles intellectual debate and hinders the development of well-rounded ideas.

Academic institutions should be spaces where diverse opinions are encouraged and debated. However, under the influence of identity politics, certain viewpoints are labeled as problematic or oppressive, effectively silencing those who hold them. This creates an environment where students and scholars are afraid to express their thoughts openly, leading to self-censorship and a lack of intellectual growth.

The Erosion of Critical Thinking

Identity politics also undermines critical thinking by promoting a binary view of the world. According to this ideology, individuals are either oppressors or oppressed based on their immutable characteristics such as race, gender, or sexuality. This simplistic framework leaves no room for nuance or complexity.

In an academic setting, critical thinking is essential for analyzing complex issues and developing innovative solutions. However, when identity politics takes center stage, critical thinking is replaced by a rigid adherence to preconceived notions. Students are discouraged from questioning the prevailing narrative and are instead expected to accept it uncritically. This not only hampers intellectual growth but also perpetuates a cycle of confirmation bias, where individuals seek out information that supports their existing beliefs.

The Loss of Intellectual Diversity

Perhaps the most concerning aspect of identity politics in academia is its detrimental effect on intellectual diversity. By prioritizing certain identities and perspectives over others, this ideology creates an environment where only a narrow range of ideas is deemed acceptable.

Intellectual diversity is crucial for fostering innovation and advancing knowledge. When individuals with different backgrounds and perspectives come together, they bring unique insights that can challenge existing paradigms and lead to groundbreaking discoveries. However, under the influence of identity politics, intellectual diversity is sacrificed in favor of ideological conformity.

The Threat to Academic Freedom

Identity politics also poses a significant threat to academic freedom. In an environment where certain ideas are deemed off-limits or taboo, scholars are discouraged from pursuing research that may challenge prevailing narratives or go against the grain.

Academic freedom is the cornerstone of any thriving intellectual community. It allows scholars to explore controversial topics, challenge established theories, and push the boundaries of knowledge. However, when identity politics takes hold, academic freedom is curtailed in favor of protecting the sensibilities of certain groups.

The Way Forward

To address the dangers posed by identity politics in academic institutions, it is crucial to promote intellectual diversity, critical thinking, and open dialogue. This requires creating an environment where all perspectives are welcomed and respected, regardless of their alignment with prevailing ideologies.

Academic institutions must prioritize the pursuit of knowledge over the promotion of any particular ideology. This means encouraging students and scholars to engage in rigorous debate, challenge existing ideas, and explore new avenues of research. It also means fostering an environment where dissenting voices are not only tolerated but actively sought out.

By embracing intellectual diversity and critical thinking, academic institutions can reclaim their role as bastions of knowledge and free inquiry. Only then can we overcome the dangers of ideological echo chambers and ensure that academia remains a space for the pursuit of truth, rather than the propagation of dogma.

Chapter 55: The Illusion of Empowerment through Identity Politics Activism

Introduction

This chapter aims to shed light on the illusion of empowerment through identity politics activism and the potential harm it can cause to individuals and society as a whole.

The Fragmentation of Society

One of the most concerning aspects of identity politics activism is its potential to fragment society. By encouraging individuals to prioritize their own identities above all else, this ideology fosters division rather than unity. Instead of working towards a common goal of equality and justice for all, identity politics activism often leads to a competition for victimhood status, where different groups vie for recognition as the most oppressed.

This fragmentation not only hinders progress but also perpetuates a cycle of resentment and animosity between different identity groups. Rather than fostering understanding and empathy, identity politics activism can create an us versus them mentality that further deepens societal divisions.

The Suppression of Individuality

Identity politics activism often places undue emphasis on group identities at the expense of individuality. While it is essential to acknowledge and address systemic inequalities faced by marginalized communities, reducing individuals to mere representatives of their identities can be dehumanizing.

By subscribing to identity politics activism, individuals may feel pressured to conform to certain expectations or ideologies associated with their group identity. This pressure can stifle individual thought and discourage dissenting opinions within these communities. The suppression of individuality undermines the very essence of personal freedom and autonomy.

The Erosion of Free Speech

Identity politics activism has also been associated with a growing intolerance towards differing viewpoints. In the pursuit of social justice, some activists have resorted to silencing or canceling individuals who express opinions that challenge their own. This erosion of free speech is deeply concerning, as it stifles open dialogue and hinders the exchange of ideas.

When certain ideas or perspectives are deemed unacceptable simply because they do not align with a particular identity group's narrative, intellectual diversity suffers. The suppression of dissenting voices not only limits our ability to critically examine and challenge prevailing beliefs but also undermines the principles of democracy and free expression.

The Perpetuation of Victimhood

While identity politics activism aims to empower marginalized communities, it can inadvertently perpetuate a victimhood mentality. By constantly emphasizing the injustices faced by specific identity groups, individuals may internalize a sense of helplessness and dependency on external validation.

This perpetuation of victimhood can hinder personal growth and resilience, as individuals may come to believe that their identities alone determine their worth and potential. Instead of encouraging individuals to overcome obstacles and strive for success, identity politics activism can inadvertently reinforce a narrative that portrays them as perpetual victims.

The Distortion of Equality

Identity politics activism often conflates equality with equity, leading to a distorted understanding of these concepts. While equality seeks to ensure fairness and equal opportunities for all individuals, equity focuses on redistributing resources based on perceived historical disadvantages.

While addressing historical injustices is crucial, the emphasis on equity can lead to a disregard for individual merit and achievement. By prioritizing group-based outcomes over individual effort, identity politics activism risks undermining the principles of fairness and meritocracy.

The Way Forward

It is essential to recognize the dangers and problems associated with identity politics activism while still acknowledging the legitimate concerns of marginalized communities. Instead of perpetuating division and victimhood, we must strive for a more inclusive and nuanced approach to social justice.

This approach should prioritize unity, individuality, and open dialogue. By fostering empathy, understanding, and respect for diverse perspectives, we can work towards a society that values both collective progress and individual autonomy.

Conclusion

The illusion of empowerment through identity politics activism must be critically examined. While this ideology may offer a sense of belonging and validation for marginalized communities, it also poses significant risks to societal cohesion, individual freedom, and intellectual diversity. It is only through a balanced and inclusive approach that we can truly achieve a just and equitable society for all.

Chapter 56: The Erosion of Rational Debate by Identity Politics Rhetoric

The Danger of Mob Mentality

One of the most significant dangers posed by identity politics is the prevalence of a mob mentality which occurs when individuals within a group prioritize consensus and conformity over critical thinking and independent analysis.

In an environment dominated by identity politics, dissenting opinions are often dismissed or silenced. Those who dare to question or challenge prevailing narratives are labeled as oppressors or bigots, effectively shutting down any meaningful debate. This stifling of dissent prevents the exploration of alternative viewpoints and hinders intellectual growth.

The Suppression of Free Speech

Identity politics also poses a significant threat to free speech. In the name of protecting marginalized groups, proponents of identity politics often advocate for the restriction of speech that they deem offensive or harmful.

While it is important to create a safe and inclusive environment for all individuals, the suppression of free speech is not the solution. By censoring certain ideas or perspectives, we risk creating an echo chamber where only one viewpoint is allowed, effectively silencing those who hold differing opinions.

The Polarization of Society

Identity politics has contributed to the increasing polarization of society. By dividing individuals into distinct identity groups, it fosters an us versus them mentality that undermines unity and cooperation.

Rather than seeking common ground and working towards shared goals, identity politics encourages individuals to view others solely through the lens of their identity. This narrow perspective hinders meaningful dialogue and prevents the formation of genuine connections between people with differing backgrounds and experiences.

The Loss of Individuality

Perhaps one of the most concerning aspects of identity politics is its tendency to reduce individuals to mere representatives of their identity group. Instead of recognizing people as unique individuals with diverse thoughts, beliefs, and experiences, identity politics reduces them to a set of predetermined characteristics.

This reductionist approach not only erases the complexity and nuance of individual identities but also undermines personal agency. It denies individuals the freedom to define themselves beyond their group affiliation and perpetuates a culture that values group identity over individual autonomy.

Conclusion

While the intentions behind identity politics may be noble, it is crucial to recognize its detrimental effects on rational debate. The erosion of rational discourse, the suppression of free speech, the polarization of society, and the loss of individuality are all alarming consequences of this ideology.

If we are to foster a society that values open dialogue, critical thinking, and genuine understanding, we must reject the divisive rhetoric of identity politics. Instead, let us embrace a more inclusive and nuanced approach that recognizes the complexity of human identities while promoting unity and respect for all.

Chapter 57: The Danger of Moral Absolutism and Intolerance in Intersectional Theory

Intersectional theory, claims to fight for equality and justice, but in reality, it promotes moral absolutism and intolerance. While it may seem appealing on the surface, we must be wary of the dangers it poses to our individual freedoms and the fabric of our society.

The Rise of Intersectional Theory

Intersectional theory originated from academia and has since gained significant traction in mainstream culture. It argues that individuals experience oppression based on their intersecting identities, such as race, gender, sexuality, and disability. While acknowledging the existence of various forms of discrimination is important, intersectional theory takes it a step further by asserting that these identities determine an individual's moral worth.

This dangerous notion creates a hierarchy of victimhood where certain groups are deemed more oppressed than others. It fosters an environment where individuals are judged solely based on their immutable characteristics rather than their actions or character. This leads to a society that values identity over individuality and perpetuates division rather than unity.

Moral Relativism vs. Moral Absolutism

One of the fundamental problems with intersectional theory is its promotion of moral absolutism. By assigning moral worth based on identity, it leaves no room for nuance or individual differences. It assumes that all members of a particular group share the same experiences and perspectives, ignoring the rich tapestry of human diversity.

This absolutist approach stifles open dialogue and critical thinking. It discourages individuals from questioning the prevailing narrative, as any dissenting opinion is labeled as oppressive or ignorant. This creates an echo chamber where only one perspective is deemed acceptable, leading to the suppression of free speech and the erosion of intellectual diversity.

The Tyranny of Intolerance

Intersectional theory claims to fight against oppression, but in reality, it often becomes the oppressor. It fosters a culture of intolerance towards those who do not conform to its rigid ideology. Dissenting voices are silenced, careers are ruined, and reputations are tarnished simply for expressing alternative viewpoints.

This intolerance extends beyond individuals and infiltrates institutions and organizations. Companies are pressured to adopt diversity quotas and prioritize identity over merit, leading to a decline in quality and competence. Academic institutions become echo chambers where only certain ideas are allowed, stifling intellectual growth and innovation.

The Threat to Individual Freedom

Perhaps the most alarming aspect of intersectional theory is its threat to individual freedom. By assigning moral worth based on identity, it denies individuals agency over their own lives. It reduces people to mere representatives of their group, stripping them of their unique experiences and aspirations.

This ideology discourages personal responsibility and self-improvement by perpetuating a victim mentality. It tells individuals that their success or failure is predetermined by their identity, leaving no room for personal growth or achievement. This not only undermines the principles of meritocracy but also hampers social progress by discouraging individual initiative.

Conclusion

While intersectional theory may claim to fight for equality and justice, its promotion of moral absolutism and intolerance poses a significant danger to our society. We must be vigilant in defending our individual freedoms and resisting the divisive and oppressive nature of this ideology. Only by embracing the principles of individuality, open dialogue, and intellectual diversity can we truly achieve a just and harmonious society.

Chapter 58: The Suppression of Artistic Freedom by Ideological Censorship

Introduction

In recent years, a dangerous trend has emerged in society - the suppression of artistic freedom by ideological censorship. This chapter aims to shed light on the alarming consequences of identity politics on the creative world. As identity ideology gains traction, artists find themselves walking on eggshells, afraid to express their true visions for fear of offending someone or being labeled as insensitive. This stifling atmosphere not only hampers artistic growth but also threatens the very essence of free expression.

The Artistic Landscape Under Siege

Art has always been a reflection of society, pushing boundaries and challenging norms. However, under the weight of identity politics, artists are forced to self-censor their work to avoid backlash or accusations of cultural appropriation. This stifling environment robs us of the vibrant diversity that art should celebrate.

The Fear of Offending

Artists are now constantly walking on eggshells, afraid to explore controversial topics or depict certain identities for fear of being labeled as insensitive or offensive. This fear stifles creativity and innovation, as artists are forced to conform to a narrow set of acceptable themes and narratives.

Art as a Catalyst for Dialogue

Art has always been a powerful tool for sparking conversations and challenging societal norms. By censoring art that may be deemed offensive, we are shutting down important dialogues that need to take place. It is through these uncomfortable conversations that we can grow as a society and foster understanding.

The Danger of Homogenization

Identity politics, in its quest for inclusivity, ironically leads to homogenization. Artists are pressured to create works that fit within the approved narratives of their respective identities, stifling individuality and diversity of thought. This homogenization not only limits artistic expression but also perpetuates stereotypes and reinforces divisions.

The Loss of Nuance

Art is a medium that thrives on nuance and complexity. However, under the influence of identity politics, nuance is often sacrificed in favor of simplistic narratives that cater to the demands of specific identity groups. This oversimplification diminishes the power of art to challenge our preconceived notions and forces us into narrow boxes.

Conclusion

The suppression of artistic freedom by ideological censorship is a dangerous trend that threatens the very essence of free expression. As identity politics continues to gain traction, artists find themselves constrained by fear and self-censorship. We must recognize the importance of allowing art to flourish in all its forms, even if it challenges our beliefs or makes us uncomfortable. Only then can we truly embrace the power of art to inspire, provoke, and foster meaningful dialogue.

Chapter 59: The Threat to Academic Integrity by Ideological Bias

The Dangers of Essentialism

One of the most troubling aspects of identity politics is its reliance on essentialism. Essentialism is the belief that certain characteristics are inherent and defining aspects of an individual's identity. This reductionist view ignores the complexity and diversity within any given group and perpetuates harmful stereotypes.

For example, proponents of identity politics often argue that all members of a particular racial or ethnic group share the same experiences and perspectives. This erases the individuality and unique experiences of each person within that group, reinforcing harmful generalizations and preventing meaningful dialogue.

Essentialism also leads to a dangerous form of tribalism, where individuals are encouraged to align themselves with their identity group and view those outside their group as adversaries. This creates an us versus them mentality that stifles intellectual growth and fosters hostility between different groups.

The Suppression of Dissenting Voices

Identity politics has also led to a chilling effect on free speech and intellectual diversity within academic institutions. Those who dare to question or challenge the prevailing narrative are often labeled as bigots, racists, or oppressors, effectively silencing any dissenting voices.

This suppression of dissent is antithetical to the principles of academic freedom and open inquiry. Universities, once bastions of free thought and intellectual exploration, have become echo chambers where only certain viewpoints are tolerated. This not only stifles innovation and critical thinking but also undermines the very purpose of higher education.

Furthermore, the suppression of dissenting voices perpetuates a dangerous cycle of confirmation bias. When only one perspective is allowed to dominate the discourse, it becomes increasingly difficult to challenge or question prevailing ideas. This leads to a stagnant intellectual environment where new ideas are dismissed without consideration.

The Erosion of Objective Standards

Identity politics also poses a threat to objective standards and meritocracy within academia. By prioritizing an individual's identity over their qualifications or achievements, identity ideology undermines the principles of fairness and equal opportunity.

For example, proponents of identity politics argue for affirmative action policies that prioritize certain groups over others in college admissions or hiring decisions. While these policies may be well-intentioned, they undermine the principle that individuals should be evaluated based on their abilities and qualifications rather than their identity.

This erosion of objective standards not only harms those who are unfairly advantaged or disadvantaged by such policies but also undermines the credibility and legitimacy of academic institutions. When individuals are selected or promoted based on their identity rather than their abilities, it undermines the pursuit of excellence and devalues the achievements of those who have worked hard to earn their positions.

The Way Forward

To preserve academic integrity and foster a truly inclusive and intellectually diverse environment, it is crucial to challenge and push back against the influence of identity politics within academia. This requires a commitment to open dialogue, critical thinking, and the free exchange of ideas.

Universities must actively promote intellectual diversity by encouraging the exploration of different perspectives and challenging prevailing ideas. They must also protect the principles of academic freedom and free speech, ensuring that all voices are heard and respected.

Additionally, it is essential to promote a more nuanced understanding of identity that recognizes the complexity and individuality of each person. By moving away from essentialism and embracing a more inclusive approach, we can foster a society that values individuals for their unique qualities rather than reducing them to mere categories.

In conclusion, the threat posed by identity politics to academic integrity cannot be underestimated. It erodes intellectual diversity, suppresses dissenting voices, and undermines objective standards. To safeguard the future of academia, we must reject this divisive ideology and embrace a more inclusive and intellectually rigorous approach.

Chapter 60: The Weaponization of Empathy as a Manipulative Tool in Intersectional Activism

The Weaponization of Empathy as a Manipulative Tool in Intersectional Activism

In recent years, a dangerous trend has emerged within the realm of identity politics - the weaponization of empathy. What was once considered a noble and compassionate trait has now been distorted and exploited as a manipulative tool in intersectional activism. This chapter aims to shed light on this alarming phenomenon and its potential consequences for society.

The Manipulative Tactics

One of the most insidious tactics employed by those who weaponize empathy is the use of emotional manipulation. By presenting their arguments through personal anecdotes and emotional appeals, they create an environment where any disagreement or critique is seen as an attack on the individual's lived experiences.

This emotional manipulation effectively shuts down rational discourse and prevents any meaningful exchange of ideas. It fosters an atmosphere where individuals are afraid to voice their opinions for fear of being labeled as insensitive or oppressive.

Furthermore, these activists often engage in what can be described as empathy shaming. They shame individuals who do not align with their views by accusing them of lacking empathy or compassion. This tactic is particularly effective in silencing dissent, as no one wants to be seen as heartless or uncaring.

The Consequences for Society

The weaponization of empathy has far-reaching consequences for society. By stifling open dialogue and discouraging dissent, it hinders the progress of social justice movements. Instead of fostering understanding and empathy between different groups, it creates an us versus them mentality, further dividing society along identity lines.

Moreover, this manipulative use of empathy undermines the very foundations of democracy and free speech. In a healthy society, individuals should be able to engage in respectful debate and challenge prevailing ideas without fear of retribution. When empathy becomes a weapon, it erodes these fundamental principles and replaces them with a culture of fear and self-censorship.

Reclaiming Empathy

It is crucial to recognize that empathy itself is not the problem; it is the manipulation and weaponization of empathy that pose a threat to our society. To combat this alarming trend, we must reclaim empathy as a force for good.

Firstly, we need to encourage open dialogue and create spaces where diverse perspectives can be shared without fear of judgment or reprisal. By fostering an environment that values respectful debate, we can ensure that empathy is used as a tool for understanding rather than as a weapon for silencing.

Secondly, we must promote critical thinking and media literacy skills. By equipping individuals with the ability to discern emotional manipulation from genuine empathy, we can empower them to navigate the complex landscape of identity politics more effectively.

Lastly, we need to emphasize the importance of empathy as a two-way street. True empathy requires not only understanding and compassion for marginalized individuals but also a willingness to listen and engage with those who hold different perspectives. By fostering empathy in all directions, we can create a more inclusive and understanding society.

Conclusion

The weaponization of empathy in intersectional activism is a concerning development that threatens the progress of social justice movements and undermines the principles of democracy. By recognizing and addressing this issue, we can reclaim empathy as a force for positive change and foster a society that values open dialogue, critical thinking, and genuine understanding.

Chapter 61: The Danger of Moral Relativism and the Erosion of Ethical Standards in Identity Politics

The Dangers of Moral Relativism

One of the most significant dangers posed by identity politics is the erosion of ethical standards through the promotion of moral relativism. Moral relativism asserts that there are no objective moral truths and that all moral judgments are subjective and dependent on individual or cultural perspectives. This rejection of universal ethical principles undermines the very foundation upon which societies are built.

When identity becomes the sole determinant of morality, it becomes impossible to hold individuals accountable for their actions. Instead of evaluating behavior based on universally accepted principles such as fairness, justice, and compassion, identity politics encourages a selective application of ethics based on group membership. This leads to a society where certain groups are exempt from criticism or consequences for their actions simply because they belong to a historically marginalized identity.

The Suppression of Dissent

Identity politics also poses a threat to free speech and intellectual diversity. In an environment where certain ideas or perspectives are deemed inherently oppressive or offensive based on the identity of the person expressing them, dissenting voices are silenced and marginalized. This stifling of debate and the suppression of alternative viewpoints is detrimental to the pursuit of truth and the advancement of knowledge.

Furthermore, the emphasis on group identities in identity politics discourages individuals from engaging in critical self-reflection and personal growth. Instead of encouraging individuals to strive for excellence and personal development, identity politics promotes a victimhood mentality where one's identity is seen as a permanent barrier to success. This not only limits individual potential but also perpetuates a cycle of victimhood and dependency.

The Polarization of Society

Identity politics has also contributed to the increasing polarization of society. By dividing people into distinct groups based on their identities, it fosters an us versus them mentality that hinders meaningful dialogue and cooperation. Instead of seeking common ground and working towards shared goals, identity politics encourages individuals to view those outside their own group as adversaries.

This polarization not only undermines social cohesion but also impedes progress on important issues such as inequality, discrimination, and social justice. By framing these complex problems solely through the lens of identity, identity politics oversimplifies the root causes and hinders effective solutions.

Conclusion

While recognizing and celebrating diversity is crucial for a just and inclusive society, it is essential to approach identity with caution. The unchecked growth of identity politics has led to a dangerous erosion of ethical standards through the promotion of moral relativism. By assigning inherent moral value to identities and suppressing dissent, identity politics undermines free speech, intellectual diversity, and personal growth. Moreover, it contributes to the polarization of society and hinders progress on important social issues. It is imperative that we critically examine the consequences of identity politics and strive for a more nuanced and inclusive approach that values both individuality and shared humanity.

Chapter 62: The Suppression of Scientific Inquiry and the Rise of Pseudoscience in Intersectional Theory

In recent years, there has been a disturbing trend in academia and society at large - the suppression of scientific inquiry and the rise of pseudoscience in intersectional theory. Intersectionality, originally a concept developed by legal scholar Kimberlé Crenshaw to examine how different forms of oppression intersect and compound each other, has been co-opted by identity ideologues to promote a dangerous and divisive agenda.

Under the guise of promoting social justice, intersectional theory has become a dogma that brooks no dissent. Any attempt to question or critically examine its tenets is met with accusations of bigotry and hate. This stifling of intellectual debate is antithetical to the principles of scientific inquiry and undermines the pursuit of truth.

The Suppression of Scientific Inquiry

One of the most troubling aspects of intersectional theory is its suppression of scientific inquiry. The dogmatic adherence to certain beliefs and narratives leaves no room for questioning or challenging prevailing ideas.

Critical analysis and rigorous debate are essential components of the scientific method. They allow for the testing and refinement of hypotheses, leading to a deeper understanding of complex phenomena. However, in the realm of intersectional theory, any dissenting voice is labeled as oppressive and silenced.

This suppression of scientific inquiry has far-reaching consequences. It hampers our ability to critically examine the validity of claims made by intersectional theorists. It prevents us from exploring alternative explanations and potential flaws in their arguments.

The Rise of Pseudoscience

In the absence of rigorous scientific inquiry, pseudoscience flourishes. Intersectional theory has become a breeding ground for unfounded claims and dubious theories that are presented as irrefutable truths.

One example of this is the concept of lived experience. Intersectional theorists argue that personal experiences are the ultimate arbiter of truth, dismissing the importance of empirical evidence and objective analysis. While personal experiences are undoubtedly valuable, they cannot be the sole basis for formulating social policies or making scientific claims.

Another pseudoscientific aspect of intersectional theory is its reliance on anecdotal evidence and cherry-picked examples to support its claims. This cherry-picking ignores the vast body of research that may contradict or complicate their narratives.

The Danger of Self-Reinforcing Thought Feedback Loops

The suppression of scientific inquiry and the rise of pseudoscience in intersectional theory create an echo chamber where dissenting voices are silenced and alternative perspectives are dismissed. This kind of feedback loop stifles innovation, hinders progress, and perpetuates a narrow-minded worldview.

When individuals are afraid to question prevailing ideas or challenge established narratives, intellectual stagnation sets in. The pursuit of truth becomes secondary to maintaining ideological purity.

Conclusion

The suppression of scientific inquiry and the rise of pseudoscience in intersectional theory pose a grave threat to intellectual freedom and the pursuit of truth. It is imperative that we reclaim the principles of scientific inquiry and foster an environment where rigorous debate and critical analysis are encouraged.

By challenging prevailing ideas and examining them through the lens of empirical evidence, we can ensure that our understanding of complex social issues is based on sound reasoning and objective analysis. Only then can we hope to address the challenges of inequality and oppression in a meaningful and effective way.

Chapter 63: The Fallacy of Collective Guilt and Innocence in Intersectional Activism

In recent years, a dangerous ideology has been gaining traction in our society - an ideology that seeks to divide us based on our identities and assign collective guilt or innocence to entire groups of people. This ideology, known as intersectional activism, claims to fight for social justice and equality, but in reality, it perpetuates a toxic cycle of blame and victimhood.

The Problem with Collective Guilt

One of the fundamental flaws of intersectional activism is its reliance on the concept of collective guilt. According to this ideology, individuals are not judged solely on their actions or character but are instead held responsible for the perceived sins of their entire identity group. This approach is not only deeply unfair but also undermines the principles of individual responsibility and accountability.

By assigning collective guilt, intersectional activists create an environment where individuals are stripped of their agency and reduced to mere representatives of their identity group. This not only erases the complexity and diversity within each group but also denies individuals the opportunity to be seen as unique human beings with their own thoughts, beliefs, and experiences.

The Danger of Collective Innocence

While intersectional activism may claim to fight against oppression, it often falls into the trap of assigning collective innocence to certain identity groups. This means that individuals belonging to these groups are automatically seen as victims who can do no wrong. By doing so, intersectional activists inadvertently perpetuate a culture of victimhood and enable a lack of personal accountability.

When collective innocence is assigned, it becomes nearly impossible to hold individuals within these groups accountable for their actions. This not only undermines the principles of justice but also perpetuates a cycle of victimhood and dependency. By absolving individuals of personal responsibility, intersectional activism hinders their growth and development, ultimately doing more harm than good.

The Erosion of Individuality

One of the most concerning aspects of intersectional activism is its tendency to erode individuality. By focusing solely on group identities, this ideology reduces individuals to mere representatives of their identity categories, ignoring their unique experiences, talents, and aspirations.

When individuals are reduced to their group identities, it becomes increasingly difficult for them to break free from the constraints imposed by intersectional activism. They are expected to conform to the narratives and expectations set by their identity group, stifling their individuality and limiting their potential for personal growth.

The Perpetuation of Division

Perhaps the most alarming consequence of intersectional activism is its role in perpetuating division within society. By constantly emphasizing differences and assigning collective guilt or innocence based on identity, this ideology fosters an us versus them mentality that hinders genuine dialogue and understanding.

Instead of promoting unity and cooperation, intersectional activism fuels animosity and resentment between different identity groups. It creates an environment where individuals are pitted against each other based on immutable characteristics rather than fostering a sense of shared humanity.

A Call for Individualism

In order to move beyond the dangers of intersectional activism, we must embrace a philosophy that values individualism over collectivism. We must recognize that each person is unique and should be judged based on their own actions and character rather than being reduced to a representative of their identity group.

By promoting individualism, we can foster a society that celebrates diversity and encourages personal responsibility. We can create an environment where individuals are empowered to pursue their own dreams and aspirations, free from the constraints imposed by collective guilt or innocence.

It is time to reject the fallacy of collective guilt and innocence in intersectional activism. Let us embrace a vision of society that values individuality, personal accountability, and genuine equality.

Chapter 64: The Weaponization of Language and the Destruction of Civil Discourse in Identity Politics

In the realm of identity politics, language has become a powerful weapon. It is no longer a tool for communication and understanding, but rather a means to divide, manipulate, and control. The rise of identity ideology has led to the destruction of civil discourse, as individuals are now more concerned with asserting their own identities and silencing opposing viewpoints than engaging in meaningful dialogue.

The Power of Words

Words have always held power. They can inspire, unite, and bring about positive change. However, in the world of identity politics, words have taken on a new role - that of weapons. Language is now used to shame, silence, and discredit those who do not conform to the prevailing narrative.

The weaponization of language begins with the manipulation of words themselves. Terms that were once innocuous or even positive have been redefined to fit the agenda of identity ideologues. For example, words like diversity and inclusion are now used to enforce conformity and stifle dissent. Those who do not adhere to the prescribed beliefs are labeled as bigots, racists, or homophobes, effectively shutting down any possibility of meaningful discussion.

Furthermore, language is used to create a hierarchy of victimhood. The more oppressed an individual claims to be, the more their words are valued and respected. This creates a perverse incentive for individuals to compete for victimhood status, leading to a culture where victimhood is celebrated rather than overcome.

The Destruction of Civil Discourse

The weaponization of language has had a devastating impact on civil discourse. Instead of engaging in thoughtful debate and discussion, individuals now resort to ad hominem attacks and character assassination. Rather than addressing the merits of an argument, identity ideologues focus on attacking the person making the argument.

This toxic environment has led to the silencing of dissenting voices. Those who dare to question or challenge the prevailing narrative are met with hostility, threats, and even violence. The fear of being labeled a bigot or facing social ostracism has created a chilling effect, where individuals self-censor their thoughts and opinions for fear of retribution.

The destruction of civil discourse is not only detrimental to individuals, but also to society as a whole. Without open and honest dialogue, progress becomes impossible. Ideas cannot be tested, refined, or improved upon if they are not allowed to be freely expressed and debated.

The Path Forward

To reclaim civil discourse and combat the weaponization of language, it is crucial that we recognize the dangers of identity politics. We must reject the notion that one's identity determines their worth or the validity of their ideas. Instead, we should focus on the content of one's arguments and engage in respectful and thoughtful debate.

Furthermore, we must resist the temptation to silence opposing viewpoints. It is only through exposure to diverse perspectives that we can challenge our own beliefs and grow intellectually. We must create spaces where individuals feel safe to express their opinions without fear of retribution.

Lastly, we must reclaim language from those who seek to use it as a weapon. We must challenge the redefinition of words and reclaim their original meanings. By doing so, we can restore language as a tool for communication and understanding, rather than a means of division and control.

Conclusion

The weaponization of language in identity politics has led to the destruction of civil discourse. It is imperative that we recognize the dangers of this trend and work towards reclaiming language and fostering open and respectful dialogue. Only then can we hope to overcome the divisive nature of identity ideology and build a more inclusive and united society.

Chapter 65: The Danger of Double Standards and Hypocrisy in Identity Politics Movements

Introduction

Identity politics movements have gained significant traction in recent years, with individuals and groups advocating for the rights and recognition of marginalized communities. While the intentions behind these movements may be noble, there is a growing concern about the dangers of double standards and hypocrisy within identity politics. This chapter aims to explore these dangers and shed light on the potential consequences of unchecked identity ideology.

The Slippery Slope of Group Identity

Identity politics often encourages individuals to define themselves primarily by their group identity, whether it be based on race, gender, sexual orientation, or any other characteristic. While it is important to acknowledge and address historical injustices faced by marginalized communities, an overemphasis on group identity can lead to a dangerous slippery slope.

When individuals are encouraged to view themselves solely through the lens of their group identity, it can foster division and animosity between different groups. This can result in a society where individuals are judged not as unique individuals but solely based on their group affiliation. Such a society risks perpetuating stereotypes, discrimination, and even violence.

The Tyranny of Double Standards

One of the most concerning aspects of identity politics is the prevalence of double standards. While proponents of identity politics often advocate for equality and fairness, they frequently engage in practices that contradict these principles.

For example, some identity politics movements argue for equal representation in various fields based on demographic characteristics such as race or gender. While diversity is undoubtedly important, it becomes problematic when it is pursued at the expense of meritocracy. When hiring decisions or promotions are based primarily on demographic factors rather than qualifications and abilities, it undermines the principles of fairness and equal opportunity.

Furthermore, identity politics often promotes the idea that certain groups should be shielded from criticism or held to different standards based on their historical oppression. While it is crucial to acknowledge and address historical injustices, it is equally important to hold all individuals and groups accountable for their actions. The selective application of standards based on group identity undermines the pursuit of justice and equality.

The Suppression of Dissenting Voices

Identity politics movements have been known to suppress dissenting voices and stifle open dialogue. This suppression often occurs under the guise of protecting marginalized communities from harm or creating safe spaces. While creating safe spaces is important, it should not come at the expense of free speech and intellectual diversity.

When individuals are afraid to express their opinions or engage in open debate due to fear of being labeled as bigots or oppressors, it hampers the progress of society. Intellectual growth and societal progress rely on the free exchange of ideas, even if those ideas may be uncomfortable or challenge prevailing beliefs.

The Danger of Tribalism

Identity politics can inadvertently foster tribalism, where individuals align themselves solely with their own group and view other groups as adversaries. This tribalistic mindset can lead to a society divided along identity lines, where cooperation and understanding become increasingly difficult.

When individuals are encouraged to prioritize their group identity over their shared humanity, it becomes challenging to find common ground and work towards a more inclusive society. The danger lies in perpetuating an us versus them mentality that hinders progress and fosters animosity between different groups.

Conclusion

While identity politics movements may have emerged with the intention of addressing historical injustices and advocating for marginalized communities, it is crucial to recognize the dangers of double standards and hypocrisy within these movements. The slippery slope of group identity, the tyranny of double standards, the suppression of dissenting voices, and the danger of tribalism all pose significant risks to societal cohesion and progress.

It is essential to approach identity politics with a critical lens, ensuring that the pursuit of justice and equality does not come at the expense of individual rights, intellectual diversity, and societal harmony. Only by acknowledging these dangers can we navigate a path towards a more inclusive and equitable society.

Chapter 66: The Suppression of Intellectual Diversity and the Decline of Academic Freedom by Cancel Culture Zealots

In recent years, a dangerous trend has emerged within academic circles and intellectual discourse. The rise of identity politics and cancel culture has led to the suppression of intellectual diversity and the erosion of academic freedom. What was once a bastion of free thought and open dialogue has now become a breeding ground for ideological conformity and the silencing of dissenting voices.

The Cancel Culture Phenomenon

Cancel culture is the weaponization of identity politics. It is the practice of publicly shaming and ostracizing individuals who express views or engage in behavior deemed unacceptable by the cancel culture zealots. This can range from social media campaigns to get someone fired from their job to boycotting businesses that do not align with their ideological beliefs.

Cancel culture operates under the guise of social justice, but in reality, it is a form of intellectual bullying. It creates an environment of fear and self-censorship, where individuals are afraid to express their opinions for fear of being targeted and labeled as bigots or oppressors.

The Suppression of Intellectual Diversity

One of the most damaging consequences of identity politics and cancel culture is the suppression of intellectual diversity. In an academic setting, the exchange of ideas and the exploration of different perspectives are crucial for intellectual growth and the advancement of knowledge.

However, in today's climate, certain topics and viewpoints are deemed off-limits. Professors and students who dare to question or challenge prevailing narratives are often met with hostility and even threats. This stifles critical thinking and hinders the pursuit of truth.

Furthermore, the pressure to conform to a particular ideology leads to groupthink. Dissenting voices are silenced or marginalized, creating an echo chamber where only one perspective is allowed. This not only limits intellectual diversity but also hampers innovation and progress.

The Erosion of Academic Freedom

Academic freedom, once a cherished principle within universities, is now under attack. Professors who hold unpopular views or engage in controversial research are increasingly at risk of losing their jobs or facing professional repercussions.

The fear of being canceled has led many academics to self-censor, avoiding certain topics or perspectives that may be deemed controversial. This self-censorship undermines the very essence of academic freedom - the ability to pursue knowledge without fear of reprisal.

Moreover, cancel culture zealots have taken it upon themselves to police academic curricula. They demand the removal of books, articles, and even entire courses that do not align with their ideological beliefs. This censorship of ideas is a direct assault on the principles of intellectual inquiry and academic freedom.

The Path Forward

To combat the suppression of intellectual diversity and the erosion of academic freedom, it is crucial that we stand up against cancel culture and identity politics. We must promote open dialogue, encourage the exploration of different perspectives, and foster an environment where dissenting voices are valued rather than silenced.

Universities and academic institutions have a responsibility to protect and uphold the principles of intellectual freedom. They must resist the pressure to conform to ideological demands and instead prioritize the pursuit of truth and knowledge.

As individuals, we must also be vigilant in defending intellectual diversity. We must challenge the prevailing narratives, engage in respectful debate, and refuse to be silenced by the fear of being canceled.

Conclusion

The suppression of intellectual diversity and the decline of academic freedom by cancel culture zealots pose a significant threat to our society. It is imperative that we recognize this danger and take action to preserve the principles that are essential for a thriving intellectual community.

Chapter 67: The Rise of Identity Politics in Corporate Culture and its Impact on Society

In recent years, a dangerous trend has been sweeping through our society, infiltrating even the most seemingly innocuous aspects of our lives. This insidious force is none other than identity politics, a divisive ideology that threatens to tear apart the very fabric of our society. Nowhere is this more evident than in the rise of identity politics within corporate culture.

The Corporate Co-opting of Identity Politics

Once confined to the realm of academia and activist circles, identity politics has now found a new home within the corporate world. Companies, eager to appear progressive and inclusive, have embraced this ideology with open arms. They have implemented diversity and inclusion programs that prioritize identity over merit, creating a toxic environment where individuals are judged not by their abilities or qualifications but by their race, gender, or other immutable characteristics.

This shift in focus has led to a dangerous erosion of meritocracy within our workplaces. Instead of rewarding hard work and talent, promotions and opportunities are now based on meeting diversity quotas. This not only undermines the principles of fairness and equality but also creates resentment among employees who feel that their achievements are being devalued in favor of superficial characteristics.

The Dangers of a Hive Mind

One of the most troubling consequences of identity politics in corporate culture is the emergence of a kind of hive mind. By prioritizing diversity over intellectual diversity, companies have inadvertently created echo chambers where dissenting opinions are silenced and conformity is rewarded.

This stifling of diverse perspectives not only hampers innovation and creativity but also poses a serious threat to free speech. Employees who dare to question the prevailing orthodoxy are labeled as bigots or oppressors, effectively silencing any meaningful debate or discussion.

This not only undermines the principles of intellectual freedom but also hinders the ability of companies to adapt and thrive in an ever-changing world.

The Rise of Victimhood Culture

Identity politics in corporate culture has also given rise to a dangerous victimhood culture. By encouraging individuals to view themselves primarily as victims of systemic oppression, companies are fostering a sense of entitlement and grievance among their employees.

This victimhood mentality not only breeds resentment and division but also undermines personal responsibility and accountability. Instead of encouraging individuals to take control of their own lives and strive for success, identity politics teaches them to blame others for their perceived disadvantages. This not only perpetuates a cycle of victimhood but also hampers the ability of individuals to overcome adversity and achieve their full potential.

The Erosion of Meritocracy

Perhaps the most alarming consequence of identity politics in corporate culture is the erosion of meritocracy. By prioritizing diversity over merit, companies are effectively lowering the bar for success and rewarding mediocrity.

This not only undermines the principles of fairness and equality but also hampers the ability of companies to compete in a global marketplace. When promotions and opportunities are based on identity rather than merit, companies are left with employees who may not have the necessary skills or qualifications to excel in their roles. This not only harms the company's bottom line but also perpetuates a cycle of mediocrity that stifles innovation and progress.

The Way Forward

It is clear that identity politics has no place within corporate culture. Companies must prioritize meritocracy over diversity quotas and create an environment where individuals are judged based on their abilities and qualifications, not their race, gender, or other immutable characteristics.

Furthermore, it is crucial that we foster a culture of intellectual diversity and open dialogue within our workplaces. By encouraging employees to express their opinions freely and respectfully engage in debate, companies can harness the power of diverse perspectives and drive innovation.

Lastly, we must reject the victimhood mentality that identity politics promotes. Instead of viewing ourselves as victims of systemic oppression, we must empower individuals to take control of their own lives and strive for success through hard work and personal responsibility.

Conclusion

The rise of identity politics in corporate culture poses a grave threat to our society. It undermines meritocracy, stifles intellectual diversity, fosters a sense of victimhood, and hampers the ability of companies to compete in a global marketplace. It is imperative that we reject this divisive ideology and work towards creating a society where individuals are judged not by their identity but by their character and abilities.

Chapter 68: The Illusion of Progress through Identity Politics Narratives: A Call to Action for a Better Future

In recent years, identity politics has gained significant traction in public discourse. Advocates argue that it is a necessary tool to address historical injustices and create a more equitable society. However, beneath the surface of this seemingly noble cause lies a dangerous ideology that threatens to undermine the very foundations of our society. This chapter aims to shed light on the dangers and problems with identity ideology, urging readers to critically examine its implications and work towards a better future.

The Fragmentation of Society

Identity politics operates on the premise that individuals should primarily be defined by their race, gender, sexual orientation, or other immutable characteristics. While it is important to acknowledge and celebrate diversity, this narrow focus on identity fragments society into competing groups, each vying for recognition and power. Instead of fostering unity and understanding, identity politics fosters division and animosity.

By reducing individuals to their group identities, identity politics erases the complexity and richness of human experience. It ignores the fact that individuals are multi-dimensional beings with unique perspectives and aspirations. This reductionist approach stifles dialogue and hinders genuine progress by pitting groups against each other in an endless battle for victimhood status.

The Suppression of Free Speech

One of the most alarming consequences of identity politics is the suppression of free speech. In an environment where certain ideas are deemed offensive or oppressive based on the identity of the speaker, open dialogue becomes impossible. Dissenting voices are silenced under the guise of protecting marginalized groups.

This suppression not only stifles intellectual growth but also creates an echo chamber where only approved narratives are allowed. It discourages critical thinking and fosters a culture of conformity, where individuals are afraid to express their opinions for fear of being labeled as bigots or oppressors. In such an environment, the marketplace of ideas becomes stagnant, and progress becomes impossible.

The Erosion of Individual Agency

Identity politics undermines the agency and autonomy of individuals by reducing them to passive victims of systemic oppression. While it is crucial to acknowledge and address systemic injustices, identity politics goes a step further by perpetuating a narrative of victimhood that denies individuals the agency to overcome their circumstances.

By framing individuals solely as victims, identity politics discourages personal responsibility and self-improvement. It fosters a culture of entitlement, where individuals believe they are owed reparations or special treatment solely based on their group identity. This mentality hinders personal growth and perpetuates a cycle of dependency on external forces for progress.

The Illusion of Progress

Identity politics creates an illusion of progress by focusing on symbolic gestures rather than substantive change. While it is important to address historical injustices and promote inclusivity, true progress requires more than just superficial representation.

Identity politics often prioritizes diversity quotas over meritocracy, leading to the promotion of individuals based on their group identity rather than their qualifications or abilities. This undermines the principles of fairness and equality that our society should strive for. True progress can only be achieved when individuals are judged based on their character and achievements rather than their immutable characteristics.

A Call to Action

It is imperative that we critically examine the dangers and problems with identity ideology. We must reject the divisive and reductionist approach of identity politics and instead work towards a society that values individuality, free speech, and personal responsibility.

To achieve this, we must foster an environment that encourages open dialogue and the free exchange of ideas. We must promote a culture of intellectual curiosity and critical thinking, where individuals are not afraid to challenge prevailing narratives.

Furthermore, we must prioritize substantive change over symbolic gestures. Instead of focusing solely on representation, we should strive for equal opportunities and a meritocratic society where individuals are judged based on their abilities rather than their group identities.

Conclusion

The dangers and problems with identity politics are clear. It fragments society, suppresses free speech, erodes individual agency, and creates an illusion of progress. It is our collective responsibility to reject this ideology and work towards a future that values unity, diversity, and genuine progress.

Chapter 69: The Myth of White Privilege

One of the most insidious aspects of this ideology is the myth of white privilege.

The concept of white privilege suggests that individuals who are white automatically have certain advantages and benefits solely based on their skin color. According to proponents of this ideology, white people are born into a world that caters to their needs and preferences, while people of color are systematically oppressed and disadvantaged.

But let's take a step back and critically examine this notion. Is it really fair to assume that all white individuals are privileged simply because of their skin color? Are we not perpetuating stereotypes and generalizations by making such sweeping claims?

The Danger of Generalizations

Identity politics relies heavily on generalizations and stereotypes. By categorizing individuals into broad groups based on their race, gender, or sexual orientation, proponents of this ideology ignore the vast diversity within these groups. Not all white people have the same experiences or opportunities, just as not all people of color face the same challenges.

By perpetuating the myth of white privilege, identity politics creates an us versus them mentality that only serves to further divide us. It fosters resentment and animosity between different racial groups instead of promoting understanding and unity.

The Individual Experience

Another flaw in the concept of white privilege is its failure to recognize the individual experiences and struggles that each person faces. It assumes that all white individuals have had an easy life, free from hardship or adversity.

But the reality is far more complex. Many white individuals come from disadvantaged backgrounds, facing poverty, abuse, or other challenges. To dismiss their struggles and assume that they have had an easy life simply because of their skin color is not only unfair but also deeply misguided.

Furthermore, the concept of white privilege ignores the achievements and successes of individuals who have worked hard to overcome obstacles and achieve their goals. It diminishes their accomplishments by attributing their success solely to their skin color rather than their hard work and determination.

The Real Issues at Stake

While identity politics focuses on divisive issues such as white privilege, it distracts us from the real problems that we should be addressing as a society. Issues such as poverty, education inequality, and systemic racism affect people of all races and should be our primary focus.

By fixating on the myth of white privilege, we lose sight of the bigger picture. We fail to address the root causes of inequality and instead engage in fruitless debates that only serve to further polarize us.

Moving Forward

It is time to reject the dangerous ideology of identity politics and move towards a more inclusive and unified society. We must recognize the individual experiences and struggles that each person faces, regardless of their race or background.

Instead of perpetuating stereotypes and generalizations, we should focus on promoting understanding, empathy, and equality for all. By working together to address the real issues at stake, we can create a society that values the uniqueness and diversity of every individual.

Let us reject the myth of white privilege and embrace a future where our identities do not define us, but rather unite us in our shared humanity.

Chapter 70: The Rise of Racism Toward White People And The Normalization Thereof

In recent years, a disturbing trend has emerged within the realm of identity politics - the rise of racism toward white people. What was once considered an abhorrent and unacceptable ideology has now been normalized and even celebrated in certain circles. This chapter aims to shed light on this dangerous phenomenon and its implications for society as a whole.

The Normalization of Anti-White Racism

One of the most alarming aspects of this shift is the normalization of anti-white racism. In the name of combating historical injustices, some proponents of identity politics have resorted to demonizing an entire racial group - white people. This dangerous rhetoric not only perpetuates stereotypes but also creates an environment where discrimination against white individuals is seen as justified.

The normalization of anti-white racism can be seen in various aspects of society. Mainstream media outlets often portray white people as inherently privileged and responsible for all societal ills. Academic institutions promote theories that argue for the inherent racism of white individuals, regardless of their personal beliefs or actions. Social media platforms are rife with hashtags and movements that openly advocate for the marginalization and exclusion of white people.

The Dangers of Anti-White Racism

The dangers of anti-white racism cannot be overstated. By perpetuating the idea that all white people are inherently racist, society risks alienating a significant portion of its population. This not only undermines efforts for unity and understanding but also creates a breeding ground for resentment and division.

Furthermore, the normalization of anti-white racism undermines the very principles that identity politics claims to uphold - equality and justice. It replaces one form of discrimination with another, perpetuating a cycle of hatred and animosity.

The Importance of Dialogue and Understanding

To address this alarming trend, it is crucial to foster open dialogue and understanding between different racial groups. Instead of demonizing one another, we must strive to recognize the complexities and nuances of individual experiences.

It is essential to acknowledge historical injustices while also recognizing that not all individuals within a racial group are responsible for those injustices. By promoting empathy and understanding, we can work towards a society that values equality and justice for all.

Conclusion

The rise of racism toward white people and its normalization within identity politics is a dangerous trend that threatens to undermine the progress made in the fight against discrimination. It is imperative that we recognize the dangers of this ideology and work towards fostering understanding and empathy between different racial groups. Only through open dialogue can we hope to create a society that truly values equality and justice for all.

Part 2: Debunking Non-Binary Gender

I want to start this Part of the book by expressing my heartfelt respect and sympathy for individuals who identify as non-binary. It is important to recognize the very real struggles that these individuals face in their lives. While I maintain that the concept of non-binary gender is a fallacy, it is crucial to separate personal beliefs from empathy and understanding.

It is undeniable that society has often failed to provide a safe and inclusive environment for those who do not conform to traditional gender norms. Non-binary individuals often encounter discrimination, misunderstanding, and marginalization. They may face challenges in accessing healthcare, education, employment, and even basic human rights. These struggles are not to be taken lightly or dismissed.

I want to emphasize that my intention is not to invalidate or belittle the experiences of those who identify as non-binary. It is essential to acknowledge their feelings and experiences as valid and real. The emotional distress caused by societal expectations and the pressure to conform can be overwhelming.
If an individual finds happiness and fulfillment in identifying as non-binary, I fully respect their position. It is their right to define themselves in a way that aligns with their personal understanding of gender. However, it is important to note that personal beliefs do not alter the objective reality of human biology.
While I extend my respect and understanding towards those who identify as non-binary, it is equally important for them to recognize that society at large may not share their beliefs. Expecting everyone to accommodate an unfounded belief (for example, by insisting that everyone use specific, made-up and meaningless pronouns) can lead to frustration and disappointment. It can also foster resentment in those finding themselves subject to such expectations.

If an individual who identifies as non-binary feels distressed by this fallacious identity, I strongly recommend seeking professional help in the form of counseling or psychotherapy. These professionals can provide guidance, support, and tools for navigating the challenges associated with gender identity.

It is my sincere hope that individuals who identify as non-binary find solace, acceptance, and happiness in their lives. I encourage them to surround themselves with a supportive community that understands and respects their journey. By fostering open dialogue and promoting education, we can work towards a society that embraces diversity while acknowledging the biological realities of gender.

In conclusion, I want to reiterate my respect and sympathy for individuals who identify as non-binary. I recognize the struggles they face and the importance of creating a more inclusive society. While I maintain that the concept of non-binary gender remains a fallacy, I believe in treating all individuals with empathy, understanding, and kindness.

Chapter 1: Introduction - Challenging the Concept of Non-Binary Gender

In recent years, there has been a growing acceptance and recognition of non-binary gender identities. Non-binary individuals identify themselves as neither exclusively male nor female, but rather as a combination or absence of both genders. This concept challenges the traditional binary understanding of gender, which categorizes individuals as either male or female based on their biological sex. However, in this book, we will argue that non-binary gender is a fallacy and that the concept of gender identity itself is problematic.

The Fallacy of Non-Binary Gender

The idea of non-binary gender rests on the assumption that there are more than two genders. Proponents argue that gender is a social construct and can be fluid, allowing for a spectrum of identities beyond male and female. However, this argument fails to acknowledge the biological reality of sex and the role it plays in shaping our understanding of gender.

Biologically, humans are classified into two distinct sexes: male and female. This classification is based on reproductive organs, chromosomes, and other physical characteristics. While there may be rare cases of intersex individuals who possess both male and female traits, these cases do not invalidate the binary nature of sex. Non-binary gender identities attempt to undermine this biological reality by suggesting that gender can exist independently of sex.

Furthermore, proponents of non-binary gender often rely on subjective experiences and personal feelings to justify their identities. While it is important to respect individuals' self-identifications, it is equally important to critically examine the validity of these claims. Without objective criteria or scientific evidence to support the existence of non-binary gender, it becomes difficult to accept it as anything more than a personal belief or preference.

The Problem with Gender Identity

The concept of gender identity itself is problematic. It suggests that one's internal sense of self can override biological reality and social expectations. While it is true that individuals may experience discomfort or distress when their gender identity does not align with societal norms, this does not negate the fact that gender is fundamentally tied to biological sex.

By divorcing gender from its biological basis, we risk erasing the experiences and struggles of those who are marginalized based on their sex. Women, for example, have historically faced discrimination and oppression due to their biological capacity for childbirth. By claiming that gender is solely a matter of personal identification, we undermine the importance of recognizing and addressing these systemic inequalities.

Furthermore, the concept of gender identity opens the door to an infinite number of possible identities, making it difficult to establish any meaningful understanding of gender. If gender can be self-defined and fluid, then it becomes impossible to create any coherent framework for understanding and addressing the unique challenges faced by different genders.

Conclusion

In this chapter, we have challenged the concept of non-binary gender and highlighted the problems with the broader notion of gender identity. The fallacy of non-binary gender lies in its disregard for biological reality and reliance on subjective experiences. By divorcing gender from its biological basis, we risk erasing the struggles faced by marginalized groups based on their sex. Furthermore, the concept of gender identity undermines any meaningful understanding of gender by allowing for an infinite number of possible identities.

In the following chapters, we will delve deeper into these arguments and explore alternative perspectives on gender that are grounded in scientific evidence and objective criteria. It is our hope that this book will contribute to a more nuanced and informed discussion on gender, ultimately leading to a better understanding of ourselves and the world we live in.

Chapter 2: The Historical and Cultural Context of Gender Identity

Introduction

In this chapter, we will explore the historical and cultural context of gender identity, with a particular focus on the fallacy of non-binary gender. By examining various societies throughout history, we will demonstrate that the concept of non-binary gender is a recent invention that lacks any substantial basis.

The Binary Nature of Gender Throughout History

Throughout recorded history, societies have consistently recognized and categorized individuals into two distinct genders: male and female. This binary understanding of gender is deeply rooted in biological differences between males and females, such as reproductive roles and physical characteristics.

Ancient civilizations, such as the Greeks and Romans, had clear distinctions between men and women. These distinctions were not merely social constructs but were based on observable biological differences. The binary nature of gender was also prevalent in indigenous cultures across the globe, where traditional roles and responsibilities were assigned based on one's biological sex.

The Rise of Non-Binary Gender in Modern Times

The concept of non-binary gender emerged relatively recently in human history, gaining traction in the late 20th century. This shift can be attributed to various social and cultural factors, including the rise of postmodernism and the influence of feminist theory.

Postmodernism, with its rejection of objective truth and embrace of subjectivity, provided fertile ground for the idea that gender is a social construct that can be detached from biological reality. This philosophical framework allowed for the questioning and deconstruction of traditional gender norms.

Feminist theory also played a significant role in promoting non-binary gender identities. Some feminists argued that traditional gender roles were oppressive and limiting, leading to the belief that individuals should be free to identify outside of the male-female binary.

The Problem with Non-Binary Gender

While the concept of non-binary gender may seem progressive and inclusive on the surface, it is fundamentally flawed and lacks any empirical basis. Non-binary gender is based on subjective feelings and self-identification rather than objective biological reality.

Furthermore, non-binary gender undermines the importance of biological sex and erases the unique experiences and struggles faced by men and women. By blurring the lines between male and female, non-binary gender diminishes the significance of biological differences that have shaped human societies for millennia.

Cultural Relativism and Non-Binary Gender

Proponents of non-binary gender often argue that gender is a social construct that varies across cultures, suggesting that non-binary identities are valid in certain societies. However, this argument fails to acknowledge that cultural practices do not determine biological reality.

While it is true that different cultures have different understandings of gender roles and expressions, these variations do not negate the binary nature of biological sex. The existence of cultural diversity does not invalidate the biological foundation of gender.

Conclusion

The historical and cultural context of gender identity reveals that non-binary gender is a fallacy lacking any substantial basis. Throughout history, societies have consistently recognized and categorized individuals into two distinct genders based on observable biological differences. The recent emergence of non-binary gender can be attributed to social and cultural factors rather than any inherent truth or validity. It is crucial to critically examine these concepts and recognize the importance of maintaining a grounded understanding of gender rooted in biological reality.

Chapter 3: The Biological Basis of Binary Sex

Introduction

In this chapter, we will explore the biological basis of binary sex and how it refutes the concept of non-binary gender. By examining the fundamental differences between male and female biology, we can debunk the myth that gender exists on a spectrum.

The Role of Chromosomes

One of the most fundamental aspects of biological sex is determined by our chromosomes. Humans typically have two sex chromosomes: XX for females and XY for males. This binary system is present in the vast majority of individuals and serves as a clear indicator of one's sex.

The presence of either XX or XY chromosomes influences the development of reproductive organs, secondary sexual characteristics, and hormonal profiles. These biological differences are not arbitrary but are deeply rooted in our genetic makeup. Thus, our gender is written into every cell of our body from our scalp to the tips of our toes.

Hormonal Profiles

Hormones play a crucial role in shaping our bodies and influencing our behavior. In males, testosterone is the primary hormone responsible for masculine traits such as increased muscle mass, facial hair growth, and a deeper voice. Females, on the other hand, have higher levels of estrogen, which contribute to breast development, wider hips, and menstruation.

The binary nature of hormonal profiles further supports the idea that there are only two distinct sexes. Non-binary gender proponents argue that individuals can have a mix of both hormones or identify with neither. However, such claims ignore the biological reality that hormone levels are predominantly determined by one's chromosomal sex.

Reproductive Organs

Another undeniable aspect of binary sex lies in our reproductive organs. Females possess ovaries, which produce eggs, while males have testes, responsible for sperm production. This clear distinction in reproductive anatomy is a direct result of our chromosomal sex.

Non-binary gender proponents often argue that intersex individuals, who possess atypical combinations of reproductive organs, prove the existence of a gender spectrum. However, intersex conditions are rare and do not negate the overwhelming binary nature of human biology.

Brain Structure and Function

Recent studies have explored potential differences in brain structure and function between males and females. While there are some variations, these differences do not support the existence of a non-binary gender spectrum.

Research has shown that certain brain regions associated with language processing and emotional regulation may differ between males and females. However, these differences are not indicative of a gender spectrum but rather reflect the complex interplay between biology and socialization.

The Fallacy of Non-Binary Gender

By examining the biological basis of binary sex, it becomes clear that non-binary gender is a fallacy. The overwhelming evidence supports the existence of only two distinct sexes: male and female. Chromosomes, hormonal profiles, reproductive organs, and brain structure all align with this binary framework.

Advocating for non-binary gender undermines the scientific understanding of human biology and perpetuates a false narrative that disregards the fundamental differences between males and females. It is essential to recognize and respect the biological reality of binary sex while acknowledging the importance of individual identity within this framework.

Conclusion

In this chapter, we have explored the biological basis of binary sex and debunked the myth of non-binary gender. The evidence overwhelmingly supports the existence of only two distinct sexes, male and female. It is crucial to base our understanding of gender on scientific facts rather than subjective interpretations. By doing so, we can foster a more accurate and informed discussion about gender identity.

Chapter 4: Debunking the Myth of Non-Binary Brain Sex

In this chapter, we will delve into the fallacy of non-binary brain sex and expose the flawed reasoning behind the concept of non-binary gender. We will explore the scientific evidence that supports the binary nature of brain sex and debunk the notion that individuals can possess a non-binary brain.

The Binary Nature of Brain Sex

The concept of brain sex refers to the idea that there are inherent differences in brain structure and function between males and females. These differences are believed to be influenced by hormones and genetics, resulting in distinct cognitive and behavioral patterns.

Numerous studies have provided compelling evidence for the binary nature of brain sex. For instance, research has consistently shown that male and female brains exhibit structural differences in areas such as the hypothalamus, amygdala, and corpus callosum. These differences contribute to variations in cognitive abilities, emotional processing, and social behavior.

Furthermore, studies using neuroimaging techniques have revealed that male and female brains display divergent patterns of activation during various tasks. For example, males tend to exhibit greater activation in regions associated with spatial reasoning, while females show increased activation in areas linked to verbal communication.

These findings strongly support the notion that brain sex is binary, with distinct characteristics associated with each gender. The idea that there could be a non-binary brain contradicts this well-established scientific understanding.

The Problem with Non-Binary Brain Sex

Advocates for non-binary gender often argue that individuals can possess a brain that does not align with traditional male or female characteristics. They claim that these individuals have a unique blend of masculine and feminine traits, resulting in a non-binary brain.

However, this argument fails to consider the complexity and diversity of human brains. While it is true that individuals may exhibit a range of cognitive and behavioral traits, these variations do not invalidate the binary nature of brain sex.

It is important to note that the existence of intersex individuals, who possess atypical combinations of male and female biological characteristics, does not support the concept of non-binary brain sex. Intersex conditions are rare and do not negate the overwhelming evidence for binary brain sex in the general population.

The Influence of Gender Identity

Another crucial aspect to consider is the influence of gender identity on brain structure and function. Gender identity refers to an individual's deeply held sense of being male, female, or something else.

Research has shown that transgender individuals, who experience a disconnect between their assigned sex at birth and their gender identity, often exhibit brain characteristics that align with their identified gender rather than their assigned sex. This suggests that gender identity plays a significant role in shaping brain development.

However, this does not support the existence of non-binary brain sex. Rather, it highlights the importance of aligning one's gender identity with their biological sex. The brain's ability to adapt and reflect an individual's gender identity does not negate the binary nature of brain sex but rather demonstrates its flexibility within the established male-female framework.

The Fallacy of Non-Binary Brain Sex

In conclusion, the concept of non-binary brain sex is a fallacy that lacks scientific evidence. The binary nature of brain sex is well-supported by numerous studies, which demonstrate distinct structural and functional differences between male and female brains.

While individuals may exhibit a range of cognitive and behavioral traits, these variations do not invalidate the binary nature of brain sex. The influence of gender identity on brain development further emphasizes the importance of aligning one's gender identity with their biological sex.

It is crucial to critically examine and debunk the myth of non-binary brain sex to ensure that society's understanding of gender remains grounded in scientific evidence. By doing so, we can foster a more informed and inclusive dialogue surrounding gender identity.

Chapter 5: The Role of Socialization in Shaping Gender Identity

Introduction

In this chapter, we will explore the role of socialization in shaping gender identity and how it relates to the fallacy of non-binary gender. We will argue that socialization plays a crucial role in reinforcing the binary nature of gender and that non-binary gender is a result of societal confusion and misguided beliefs.

Socialization and Gender Norms

From an early age, individuals are socialized into specific gender roles based on their biological sex. Society imposes expectations and norms on individuals, dictating how they should behave, dress, and express themselves based on their assigned gender. This socialization process reinforces the binary understanding of gender, where individuals are expected to conform to either male or female roles.

Non-binary gender challenges this binary understanding by claiming that individuals can exist outside of these traditional categories. However, this notion disregards the powerful influence of socialization in shaping our understanding of gender identity.

The Influence of Socialization on Gender Identity

Socialization begins at birth and continues throughout our lives. It shapes our beliefs, attitudes, and behaviors, including our understanding of gender. From childhood, we are bombarded with messages that reinforce the binary nature of gender. Toys, clothing, media, and even language all contribute to this process.

Children are taught what is considered appropriate behavior for their assigned gender. Boys are encouraged to be assertive, competitive, and tough, while girls are expected to be nurturing, passive, and emotional. These societal expectations heavily influence how individuals perceive themselves and others in relation to gender.

Non-binary gender challenges these societal expectations by suggesting that individuals can reject or transcend these norms. However, this rejection of societal norms does not invalidate the binary nature of gender. It simply reflects an individual's personal beliefs and preferences, rather than a fundamental truth about gender identity.

The Fallacy of Non-Binary Gender

Non-binary gender is a fallacy because it fails to recognize the powerful influence of socialization in shaping our understanding of gender. While individuals may feel a disconnect from traditional gender roles, this does not negate the binary nature of gender itself.

Furthermore, non-binary gender lacks a clear definition and consistent understanding. It is often used as an umbrella term for various identities that do not fit within the male or female categories. This lack of clarity further undermines the validity of non-binary gender as a distinct and coherent concept.

Conclusion

In conclusion, socialization plays a significant role in shaping our understanding of gender identity. The binary nature of gender is deeply ingrained in society through socialization processes that begin at birth. Non-binary gender challenges this binary understanding but fails to provide a coherent and consistent alternative. It is essential to recognize the fallacy of non-binary gender and acknowledge the powerful influence of socialization in shaping our perception of gender.

Chapter 6: Understanding the Psychological Factors Behind Non-Binary Gender Identity

Introduction

In this chapter, we will delve into the psychological factors that contribute to the emergence of non-binary gender identity. By understanding these factors, we can better comprehend why non-binary gender is a fallacy and debunk the myth surrounding it.

The Influence of Social Constructs

One of the primary psychological factors behind non-binary gender identity is the influence of social constructs. Society has constructed a binary understanding of gender, categorizing individuals as either male or female. However, some individuals may feel restricted by these categories and seek to identify outside of them.

While it is understandable that individuals may question societal norms, it is important to recognize that non-binary gender is not a valid alternative. It is merely a rejection of the established binary system without offering a coherent alternative.

Psychological Distress and Identity Confusion

Another psychological factor that contributes to non-binary gender identity is psychological distress and identity confusion. Some individuals may experience discomfort with their assigned gender or struggle with their sense of self.

However, it is crucial to approach these experiences with caution and not jump to the conclusion that non-binary gender is a valid solution. Psychological distress and identity confusion are complex issues that require proper evaluation and support from mental health professionals, rather than embracing an unsupported concept like non-binary gender.

The Role of Attention-Seeking Behavior

Attention-seeking behavior can also play a role in the emergence of non-binary gender identity. Some individuals may adopt non-binary identities as a means to gain attention or stand out from the crowd.

While it is important to acknowledge and address the underlying issues that drive attention-seeking behavior, validating non-binary gender as a legitimate identity only perpetuates the fallacy. It is essential to focus on promoting healthy ways of seeking attention and addressing the root causes of this behavior, rather than embracing unsupported concepts.

The Influence of Peer Pressure

Peer pressure can be a significant psychological factor behind non-binary gender identity. In an attempt to fit in or gain acceptance within certain social circles, individuals may adopt non-binary identities.

However, it is crucial to recognize that peer pressure should not dictate one's understanding of gender. Validating non-binary gender based on peer pressure undermines the importance of critical thinking and individual autonomy.

The Desire for Special Treatment

Lastly, the desire for special treatment can also contribute to the emergence of non-binary gender identity. Some individuals may adopt non-binary identities in order to receive unique accommodations or privileges.

However, it is important to address this desire for special treatment through fair and equal treatment for all individuals, rather than endorsing unsupported concepts like non-binary gender. Treating everyone with respect and dignity should not be contingent upon adopting a fallacious understanding of gender.

Conclusion

By examining the psychological factors behind non-binary gender identity, we can clearly see that it is a fallacy. Social constructs, psychological distress, attention-seeking behavior, peer pressure, and the desire for special treatment all contribute to the emergence of non-binary gender identity. However, it is crucial to approach these factors with skepticism and promote critical thinking rather than embracing unsupported concepts. Non-binary gender is not a valid alternative to the established binary system and should be debunked as a myth.

Chapter 7: The Problem with Self-Diagnosis and Self-Identification

Introduction

In this chapter, we will explore the problematic nature of self-diagnosis and self-identification when it comes to non-binary gender. While it is important to respect individuals' autonomy and self-expression, it is equally crucial to critically examine the validity and consequences of self-identifying as non-binary. We will delve into the potential pitfalls and implications of self-diagnosis, highlighting the need for a more rigorous and objective approach to understanding gender.

The Subjectivity of Self-Diagnosis

One of the fundamental issues with self-diagnosis is its inherent subjectivity. When individuals self-identify as non-binary, they are essentially diagnosing themselves without any external validation or professional assessment. This lack of objectivity raises concerns about the accuracy and reliability of such diagnoses.

Unlike medical conditions that can be objectively diagnosed through tests and examinations, non-binary gender is a deeply personal and subjective experience. It cannot be measured or quantified in the same way as physical ailments or mental disorders. Therefore, relying solely on self-diagnosis for non-binary gender undermines the credibility of this identity.

The Influence of Social Factors

Another problem with self-identification as non-binary is the potential influence of social factors. Society plays a significant role in shaping our understanding of gender, and individuals may feel compelled to identify as non-binary due to external pressures or trends.

The rise in visibility and acceptance of non-binary identities has undoubtedly created a cultural climate where identifying outside the traditional binary is seen as progressive and enlightened. However, this societal influence can lead to individuals adopting non-binary identities without fully understanding or experiencing the complexities associated with them.

Self-identification based on social factors rather than genuine personal experiences undermines the integrity of non-binary gender as a valid identity. It blurs the line between genuine self-discovery and conforming to societal expectations.

The Lack of Objective Criteria

Unlike binary gender identities, which are based on observable biological characteristics, non-binary gender lacks objective criteria for identification. This absence of clear guidelines or markers makes it difficult to determine what qualifies as non-binary.

Without objective criteria, self-identification becomes a subjective exercise that relies solely on an individual's perception and interpretation of their own experiences. This subjectivity opens the door for misinterpretation, confusion, and potential misuse of the non-binary label.

Furthermore, the lack of objective criteria hampers scientific research and understanding of non-binary gender. Without clear parameters, it becomes challenging to conduct meaningful studies or gather reliable data on the prevalence and nature of non-binary identities.

The Potential for Misdiagnosis

Self-diagnosis also raises concerns about misdiagnosis and the potential for individuals to inaccurately identify as non-binary. Without external validation or professional guidance, individuals may misinterpret their feelings or experiences, leading to a misdiagnosis that can have long-lasting consequences.

Misdiagnosis not only affects the individual but also impacts broader discussions around gender identity. It can perpetuate misunderstandings and misconceptions about non-binary gender, further complicating efforts to foster understanding and acceptance.

Conclusion

While self-identification is an essential aspect of personal autonomy and self-expression, it is crucial to critically examine its implications in the context of non-binary gender. The subjective nature of self-diagnosis, the influence of social factors, the lack of objective criteria, and the potential for misdiagnosis all contribute to the problematic nature of self-identification as non-binary.

To foster a more comprehensive understanding of gender, it is necessary to move beyond self-diagnosis and embrace a more rigorous and objective approach. By doing so, we can ensure that discussions around non-binary gender are grounded in evidence and promote genuine understanding and acceptance.

Chapter 8: Examining the Flaws in Non-Binary Gender Theory

Introduction

In this chapter, we will critically examine the flaws in non-binary gender theory. We will delve into the inconsistencies and contradictions that undermine the validity of non-binary gender and challenge the notion that it is a legitimate identity. By doing so, we aim to debunk the myth of non-binary gender and shed light on the problematic nature of gender identity.

The Binary Nature of Biological Sex

One of the fundamental flaws in non-binary gender theory lies in its disregard for the binary nature of biological sex. Science has long established that humans are born with either male or female reproductive systems, determined by their chromosomes. This binary distinction is rooted in our biology and cannot be ignored or dismissed.

Non-binary gender proponents argue that gender is a social construct separate from biological sex. However, this argument fails to acknowledge that gender identity is often based on biological sex. The majority of individuals identify as either male or female, aligning with their biological sex. Non-binary gender, therefore, contradicts this natural binary framework.

Lack of Consistency in Non-Binary Gender Definitions

Another flaw in non-binary gender theory is the lack of consistency in its definitions. Non-binary gender is often described as an umbrella term encompassing various identities outside the male-female binary. However, there is no clear consensus on what these identities entail.

Some individuals who identify as non-binary may experience fluidity in their gender expression or may reject traditional gender norms. Others may feel a disconnect from both masculinity and femininity. With such a wide range of interpretations, it becomes challenging to define and understand what non-binary gender truly means.

This lack of consistency undermines the credibility of non-binary gender as a valid identity. Without clear and coherent definitions, it becomes difficult to engage in meaningful discussions or research on the topic.

Contradictions with Gender Identity

Non-binary gender theory also faces contradictions when examined in relation to the concept of gender identity itself. Proponents argue that gender identity is an innate sense of self, independent of biological sex. However, if gender identity is truly separate from biological sex, then why does non-binary gender rely on the existence of a binary framework?

By identifying as non-binary, individuals are still defining their gender in relation to the male-female binary. This contradiction suggests that non-binary gender is not a distinct identity but rather an attempt to reject or challenge traditional gender norms within the existing binary framework.

Implications for Society

The flaws in non-binary gender theory have significant implications for society. By promoting the idea that individuals can exist outside the male-female binary, non-binary gender theory undermines the stability and coherence of traditional gender roles and expectations.

This destabilization can lead to confusion and uncertainty, particularly for young people who are still developing their sense of self. It may also create challenges in areas such as healthcare, education, and legal frameworks that rely on a binary understanding of gender.

Conclusion

In conclusion, the flaws in non-binary gender theory are evident when critically examined. The disregard for the binary nature of biological sex, lack of consistency in definitions, contradictions with gender identity, and implications for society all contribute to debunking the myth of non-binary gender.

It is crucial to recognize that gender identity should not be based on personal feelings or societal constructs but grounded in biological reality. By acknowledging the binary nature of biological sex, we can foster a more accurate understanding of gender and promote a healthier society.

Chapter 9: The Inconsistencies in Non-Binary Gender Terminology

Introduction

In this chapter, we will explore the inconsistencies that arise from the use of non-binary gender terminology. While proponents of non-binary gender argue that it is a valid and necessary identity, a closer examination reveals numerous contradictions and inconsistencies that undermine its credibility. By critically analyzing the language and concepts associated with non-binary gender, we can debunk the myth and expose the problem with gender identity.

The Problem with Non-Binary

The very term non-binary implies a negation of binary gender, suggesting that there are only two distinct categories: male and female. However, this oversimplification fails to acknowledge the rich diversity of human experiences and identities. By reducing gender to a binary framework, non-binary proponents inadvertently reinforce the very system they claim to reject.

The Fallacy of Genderqueer

Another commonly used term within the non-binary community is genderqueer. This label attempts to capture a sense of fluidity and ambiguity in one's gender identity. However, by combining the words gender and queer, proponents of this term inadvertently perpetuate confusion and undermine their own argument.

The term queer historically refers to sexual orientation rather than gender identity. By conflating these two distinct aspects of human experience, non-binary advocates muddy the waters and make it difficult to have meaningful discussions about either topic. This inconsistency further weakens the case for non-binary gender as a legitimate identity.

The Contradiction of Genderfluid

One of the most perplexing terms used within the non-binary community is genderfluid. This label suggests that an individual's gender identity can change over time, fluctuating between male, female, or other identities. However, this concept directly contradicts the fundamental premise of non-binary gender.

If non-binary gender is defined as existing outside of the binary framework, then how can one simultaneously identify as non-binary and experience shifts between binary genders? This contradiction exposes the inherent flaws in the concept of non-binary gender and raises questions about its validity.

The Absurdity of Demigender

One of the more recent additions to the lexicon of non-binary gender is the term demigender. This label is used to describe individuals who partially identify with a particular gender while also identifying as non-binary. However, this concept is inherently contradictory.

If one identifies as non-binary, they are explicitly rejecting the notion of belonging to any specific gender category. By claiming to be partially aligned with a particular gender while also identifying as non-binary, individuals who use this term undermine their own argument and contribute to the confusion surrounding gender identity.

The Fallacy of Agender

The term agender is often used within the non-binary community to describe individuals who do not identify with any gender. While proponents argue that this label represents a valid identity, it fails to withstand critical scrutiny.

If one truly does not identify with any gender, then why adopt a label that defines them in relation to gender? The use of the term agender paradoxically reinforces the very concept it claims to reject. This inconsistency highlights the inherent problems with non-binary gender terminology.

Conclusion

The inconsistencies in non-binary gender terminology undermine its credibility as a valid identity. By reducing gender to a binary framework, perpetuating confusion through language, and contradicting the fundamental premise of non-binary gender, proponents of this concept inadvertently weaken their own argument. It is essential to critically examine the language and concepts associated with non-binary gender to debunk the myth and expose the problem with gender identity.

Chapter 10: The Impact of Non-Binary Gender on Traditional Feminism

Introduction

In this chapter, we will explore the impact of non-binary gender on traditional feminism. We will argue that the concept of non-binary gender undermines the goals and principles of feminism, ultimately diluting its power and effectiveness. By challenging the validity of non-binary gender, we aim to restore the focus on women's rights and address the problematic consequences of embracing a fluid and subjective understanding of gender.

Reinforcing Gender Stereotypes

One of the fundamental tenets of feminism is to challenge and dismantle gender stereotypes that limit women's opportunities and perpetuate inequality. However, the concept of non-binary gender inadvertently reinforces these very stereotypes. By suggesting that individuals can exist outside the binary categories of male and female, non-binary gender inadvertently implies that certain traits or behaviors are inherently masculine or feminine. This reinforces harmful stereotypes and undermines efforts to break free from traditional gender roles.

Diverting Attention from Women's Issues

Feminism has long been focused on addressing the unique challenges faced by women in a patriarchal society. However, the rise of non-binary gender has shifted the conversation away from women's issues towards a broader discussion on gender identity. While it is important to recognize and respect diverse experiences, it should not come at the expense of prioritizing women's rights. By diverting attention from women's issues, non-binary gender dilutes the feminist movement's impact and hinders progress towards achieving gender equality.

Undermining Legal Protections for Women

Legal protections for women have been hard-fought victories for feminists throughout history. However, embracing non-binary gender poses a threat to these hard-won gains. By blurring the lines between male and female, non-binary gender challenges the legal frameworks that have been put in place to protect women's rights. This can have serious consequences, such as eroding protections against gender-based violence or undermining affirmative action policies aimed at addressing historical gender disparities.

Erasing the Experiences of Women

Feminism seeks to amplify the voices and experiences of women, who have historically been marginalized and silenced. However, the concept of non-binary gender risks erasing the specific experiences of women by collapsing gender into a subjective and individualistic construct. By prioritizing individual identity over shared experiences, non-binary gender undermines the collective struggle for women's rights and perpetuates a culture of invisibility for women.

Conclusion

Non-binary gender poses significant challenges to traditional feminism. By reinforcing gender stereotypes, diverting attention from women's issues, undermining legal protections for women, and erasing their experiences, non-binary gender dilutes the power and effectiveness of feminism. It is crucial to critically examine the impact of non-binary gender on feminism and ensure that the focus remains on advancing women's rights and achieving true gender equality.

Chapter 11: Non-Binary Gender and its Effect on LGBTQ+ Activism

In this chapter, we will explore the impact of non-binary gender on LGBTQ+ activism and argue that it undermines the movement's goals and dilutes its message. Non-binary gender, as we have established throughout this book, is a fallacy that lacks scientific evidence and logical coherence. By promoting the idea that gender exists on a spectrum beyond the binary, activists inadvertently perpetuate harmful stereotypes and hinder progress towards true equality.

The Problem with Inclusivity

One of the main arguments put forth by proponents of non-binary gender is that it promotes inclusivity within the LGBTQ+ community. They argue that by recognizing and validating non-binary identities, we create a more accepting and diverse society. However, this argument fails to consider the consequences of such inclusivity.

By expanding the definition of gender to include an infinite number of identities, we risk diluting the focus of LGBTQ+ activism. The movement was originally founded to fight for the rights and recognition of individuals who do not conform to traditional gender norms. By broadening the definition of gender to include everyone, regardless of their conformity to societal expectations, we lose sight of the original purpose of the movement.

Furthermore, by including non-binary identities within the LGBTQ+ umbrella, we inadvertently perpetuate harmful stereotypes about gender. Non-binary individuals are often portrayed as confused or attention-seeking, reinforcing the idea that their identity is not valid or deserving of respect. This undermines the progress made in challenging traditional gender roles and reinforces harmful societal norms.

The Erosion of Biological Reality

Another consequence of promoting non-binary gender is the erosion of biological reality. Gender is not simply a social construct; it is rooted in biological differences between male and female bodies. By denying the binary nature of gender, we deny the biological realities that underpin it.

This denial of biological reality has far-reaching implications. It undermines the scientific understanding of sex and gender, which is crucial for medical research and healthcare. It also erases the experiences of individuals who have undergone gender-affirming surgeries or hormone treatments to align their bodies with their gender identity.

Furthermore, by promoting non-binary gender, we risk reinforcing harmful stereotypes about masculinity and femininity. By suggesting that these categories are fluid and subjective, we undermine the progress made in challenging rigid gender roles and expectations.

The Impact on Transgender Individuals

Lastly, the promotion of non-binary gender can have a detrimental impact on transgender individuals. Transgender individuals have long fought for recognition and acceptance within society. By promoting non-binary gender as a valid identity, we risk overshadowing the struggles faced by transgender individuals who identify strictly as male or female.

Transgender individuals often face discrimination and violence due to their gender identity. By diluting the focus on transgender issues with non-binary identities, we risk diverting resources and attention away from the specific needs of transgender individuals.

Conclusion

In conclusion, non-binary gender undermines LGBTQ+ activism by diluting its focus, eroding biological reality, perpetuating harmful stereotypes, and overshadowing the struggles faced by transgender individuals. While inclusivity is an important goal, it should not come at the expense of clarity and progress towards true equality. It is crucial that we critically examine the validity of non-binary gender and its impact on LGBTQ+ activism to ensure that our efforts are focused on achieving meaningful change.

Chapter 12: The Dangers of Pseudoscience in Non-Binary Gender Discourse

Introduction

In this chapter, we will explore the dangers of pseudoscience in non-binary gender discourse. Pseudoscience refers to theories or beliefs that are presented as scientific but lack empirical evidence or rigorous scientific methodology. Unfortunately, the non-binary gender movement has been heavily influenced by pseudoscientific ideas, which not only undermine the credibility of the movement but also pose significant risks to individuals who identify as non-binary.

The Problem with Non-Binary Gender as a Scientific Concept

Non-binary gender is often presented as a scientifically valid concept, but upon closer examination, it becomes clear that it lacks a solid foundation in scientific research. The idea that there are more than two genders is based on subjective experiences and personal feelings rather than objective evidence.

Furthermore, proponents of non-binary gender often rely on anecdotal evidence and cherry-picked studies to support their claims. This selective use of evidence undermines the scientific integrity of the argument and leads to biased conclusions.

The Role of Confirmation Bias in Non-Binary Gender Discourse

Confirmation bias is a cognitive bias that leads individuals to interpret information in a way that confirms their preexisting beliefs or hypotheses. In the context of non-binary gender discourse, confirmation bias plays a significant role in perpetuating pseudoscientific ideas.

Individuals who identify as non-binary may actively seek out information that supports their gender identity while dismissing or ignoring evidence that contradicts it. This selective attention to information reinforces their belief in non-binary gender and prevents them from critically evaluating the validity of their own experiences.

The Influence of Social Constructionism on Non-Binary Gender

Social constructionism is a theoretical framework that argues that gender is a social construct rather than a biological or innate characteristic. While social constructionism has contributed valuable insights to our understanding of gender, it has also been misused to support pseudoscientific claims about non-binary gender.

Proponents of non-binary gender often argue that because gender is socially constructed, individuals can choose their gender identity freely. However, this argument ignores the biological and psychological factors that influence gender identity and oversimplifies the complex nature of human identity.

The Risks of Pseudoscience in Non-Binary Gender Discourse

The uncritical acceptance of pseudoscientific ideas in non-binary gender discourse poses several risks to individuals who identify as non-binary. Firstly, it can lead to the medicalization of gender identity, where individuals seek unnecessary medical interventions to align their bodies with their perceived gender identity.

Secondly, the reliance on pseudoscience can undermine the credibility of the non-binary gender movement as a whole. When non-binary gender is presented as a scientifically valid concept without sufficient evidence, it opens the door for criticism and skepticism from those who are not convinced by pseudoscientific arguments.

Conclusion

Pseudoscience has no place in non-binary gender discourse. It undermines the credibility of the movement and poses risks to individuals who identify as non-binary. It is essential to critically evaluate the scientific validity of claims about non-binary gender and rely on rigorous research methods to ensure that our understanding of gender is based on evidence rather than personal beliefs or subjective experiences.

Chapter 13: The Intersectionality Debate and Non-Binary Gender Identity

Introduction

In this chapter, we will explore the intersectionality debate and its relationship to the concept of non-binary gender identity. Intersectionality, a term coined by Kimberlé Crenshaw, refers to the interconnected nature of social categorizations such as race, class, and gender as they apply to an individual or group. While intersectionality has been instrumental in highlighting the experiences of marginalized communities, it is important to critically examine how it intersects with non-binary gender identity.

The Fallacy of Non-Binary Gender Identity

Before delving into the intersectionality debate, it is crucial to reiterate that non-binary gender identity itself is a fallacy. As discussed in previous chapters, gender is a binary construct rooted in biological differences between male and female. Non-binary gender identity attempts to undermine this fundamental truth by asserting that individuals can exist outside of this binary framework. However, there is no scientific evidence to support the existence of non-binary genders.

Intersectionality and Marginalized Communities

Intersectionality has played a vital role in shedding light on the unique challenges faced by marginalized communities. By recognizing that individuals can experience multiple forms of oppression simultaneously, intersectionality has helped advocate for social justice and equality. It has been particularly effective in addressing issues related to race and gender.

The Problem with Applying Intersectionality to Non-Binary Gender Identity

While intersectionality has been valuable in understanding the experiences of marginalized communities, applying it to non-binary gender identity poses significant problems. Non-binary gender identity is not an inherent characteristic like race or socioeconomic status; rather, it is a subjective self-identification that lacks empirical evidence. By equating non-binary gender identity with other forms of oppression, intersectionality inadvertently legitimizes a concept that is fundamentally flawed.

Intersectionality and the Erosion of Biological Reality

One of the dangers of applying intersectionality to non-binary gender identity is the erosion of biological reality. Intersectionality acknowledges the importance of recognizing and addressing systemic inequalities based on race, class, and other social categories. However, when it comes to gender, intersectionality blurs the line between biological differences and self-identified identities.

The Impact on Women's Rights

Another consequence of applying intersectionality to non-binary gender identity is the potential impact on women's rights. Women have historically been marginalized and oppressed based on their biological sex. By including non-binary gender identities within the framework of intersectionality, there is a risk of diluting the specific struggles faced by women and undermining efforts to achieve gender equality.

Conclusion

While intersectionality has been instrumental in addressing systemic inequalities, it is important to critically examine its application to non-binary gender identity. Non-binary gender identity lacks scientific evidence and undermines the binary nature of gender. By equating it with other forms of oppression, intersectionality inadvertently legitimizes a fallacious concept. It is crucial to separate legitimate struggles from subjective self-identifications in order to maintain clarity and promote genuine social progress.

Chapter 14: Analyzing the Role of Privilege in Non-Binary Gender Discourse

Introduction

In this chapter, we will delve into the role of privilege in non-binary gender discourse. It is essential to critically examine the privileges that individuals claiming non-binary gender identities may possess and how these privileges impact the validity of their claims. By doing so, we can better understand the fallacy of non-binary gender and the problematic nature of gender identity as a whole.

Privilege and Non-Binary Gender

Privilege plays a significant role in shaping the discourse around non-binary gender. Those who claim non-binary identities often come from privileged backgrounds, where they have the luxury to explore and experiment with their gender identity without facing severe consequences. This privilege allows them to engage in a discourse that is detached from the realities faced by marginalized communities.

Access to Resources

Individuals claiming non-binary gender often have access to resources such as education, healthcare, and support networks that enable them to navigate their identity journey more comfortably. This access to resources sets them apart from those who lack such privileges and are unable to explore their gender identity freely. It is crucial to acknowledge that this privilege influences their understanding and perception of non-binary gender.

Intersectionality and Non-Binary Gender

Intersectionality, the interconnected nature of social categorizations such as race, class, and gender, further highlights the privilege inherent in non-binary gender discourse. Those who claim non-binary identities often belong to privileged social groups, which allows them to navigate their gender identity within a more accepting and accommodating environment. This intersectionality of privilege further undermines the validity of non-binary gender.

Co-opting Marginalized Experiences

Non-binary gender discourse often co-opts the experiences of marginalized communities, such as transgender individuals and people of color. By claiming a non-binary identity, individuals may inadvertently overshadow and erase the struggles faced by these communities. This co-optation is a manifestation of privilege and further demonstrates the fallacy of non-binary gender.

Conclusion

Analyzing the role of privilege in non-binary gender discourse reveals the fallacy behind this concept. Privilege allows individuals to explore their gender identity without facing severe consequences and co-opt marginalized experiences. The focus on individual identity detracts from addressing systemic issues and perpetuates a problematic understanding of gender. It is essential to critically examine these privileges to debunk the myth of non-binary gender and challenge the problematic nature of gender identity as a whole.

Chapter 15: The Problematic Nature of Non-Binary Pronouns

Introduction

In this chapter, we will delve into the problematic nature of non-binary pronouns. Pronouns are an essential part of language, used to refer to individuals and establish their gender identity. However, the concept of non-binary pronouns challenges the traditional binary understanding of gender, leading to confusion and undermining the linguistic foundation of our society.

The Importance of Pronouns

Pronouns play a crucial role in communication, allowing us to refer to individuals without constantly using their names. They provide a convenient way to address someone or talk about them in their absence. Pronouns have historically been based on a binary understanding of gender, with he for males and she for females.

This binary system has worked effectively for centuries, allowing for clear and concise communication. It is deeply ingrained in our language and culture, providing a sense of stability and familiarity. Non-binary pronouns disrupt this established system, creating confusion and hindering effective communication.

The Fallacy of Non-Binary Gender

Before delving into the problematic nature of non-binary pronouns, it is important to reiterate that non-binary gender itself is a fallacy. The idea that individuals can exist outside the traditional male-female binary is unsupported by scientific evidence and contradicts the biological reality of human reproduction.

Gender is not a social construct but rather a biological fact determined by chromosomes and reproductive anatomy. Non-binary gender attempts to undermine this fundamental truth by suggesting that individuals can choose or identify as something other than male or female. Such claims lack scientific basis and should be treated as mere personal beliefs rather than objective reality.

Confusion and Ambiguity

One of the main problems with non-binary pronouns is the confusion and ambiguity they introduce into language. Pronouns are meant to provide clarity and facilitate effective communication, but non-binary pronouns often have no clear definition or consistent usage.

Unlike traditional pronouns, which have a well-established meaning, non-binary pronouns can vary greatly from person to person. Some individuals may prefer they/them while others may choose entirely new pronouns such as ze/zir or xe/xem. This lack of standardization makes it difficult for others to understand and use these pronouns correctly.

Furthermore, non-binary pronouns often require individuals to constantly explain and educate others about their preferred pronouns. This places an unnecessary burden on both the speaker and the listener, detracting from the primary purpose of communication - conveying information efficiently.

Undermining Linguistic Foundations

Non-binary pronouns also undermine the linguistic foundations of our society. Language evolves naturally over time, but it is rooted in established structures and conventions that allow for effective communication. Non-binary pronouns challenge these structures by introducing new words and grammatical rules that deviate from traditional usage.

This deviation creates a fracture in our linguistic framework, making it harder for individuals to understand and communicate with one another. It also places an undue burden on society to adapt to these new pronouns, requiring changes in grammar rules, dictionaries, and educational materials.

The Slippery Slope of Pronoun Proliferation

The introduction of non-binary pronouns opens the door to a slippery slope of pronoun proliferation. If we accept the idea that individuals can choose their own pronouns based on personal identity, where do we draw the line?

If non-binary pronouns are valid, then why not allow individuals to create their own unique pronouns? This would lead to an endless array of pronouns, making communication increasingly difficult and convoluted. It would also undermine the purpose of pronouns as a tool for efficient and effective communication.

Conclusion

Non-binary pronouns are problematic for several reasons. They introduce confusion and ambiguity into language, undermine the linguistic foundations of our society, and open the door to a slippery slope of pronoun proliferation. It is essential to recognize the fallacy of non-binary gender and maintain the traditional binary understanding of gender and pronouns for the sake of clear and effective communication.

Chapter 16: Examining the Impact of Non-Binary Gender on Language and Communication

Language and communication are fundamental aspects of human society. They shape our understanding of the world and how we interact with one another. However, the rise of non-binary gender has had a significant impact on language and communication, leading to confusion and a breakdown in effective communication.

The concept of non-binary gender suggests that there are more than two genders, and that individuals can identify as something other than male or female. This goes against the traditional understanding of gender as a binary system, where individuals are either male or female. By introducing non-binary gender into our language and communication, we are forced to question the very foundations of our understanding of gender.

The Problem with Pronouns

One of the most noticeable impacts of non-binary gender on language is the introduction of new pronouns. Instead of using he or she, individuals who identify as non-binary may prefer to be referred to as they or them. This creates confusion and ambiguity in communication.

Using plural pronouns to refer to an individual can lead to misunderstandings and misinterpretations. It becomes difficult to determine whether someone is referring to a single person or a group of people. This confusion hinders effective communication and can lead to frustration for both the speaker and the listener.

Furthermore, the introduction of new pronouns adds unnecessary complexity to our language. English already has a well-established system of pronouns that have been used for centuries. By introducing new pronouns for non-binary individuals, we are creating an unnecessary burden on society to learn and adapt to these changes.

The Erosion of Gendered Language

Another impact of non-binary gender on language is the erosion of gendered language. Traditionally, certain words and phrases have been associated with specific genders. For example, actor has been used to refer to a male performer, while actress has been used to refer to a female performer.

However, with the rise of non-binary gender, there is a push to use gender-neutral language that does not reinforce traditional gender roles. While this may seem like a positive step towards inclusivity, it actually erodes the richness and diversity of our language.

Language is a reflection of our culture and history. It is through language that we express our identities and experiences. By removing gendered language, we are stripping away an important aspect of our cultural heritage.

The Slippery Slope of Language

The impact of non-binary gender on language goes beyond pronouns and gendered language. It opens the door to a slippery slope where any word or phrase can be questioned and deemed offensive or exclusionary.

For example, the term mother traditionally refers to a female parent. However, with the rise of non-binary gender, there are those who argue that the term should be inclusive of individuals who do not identify as female but still fulfill the role of a parent. This leads to confusion and dilutes the meaning of the word.

If we continue down this path, where any word or phrase can be questioned and changed based on individual preferences, our language will become fragmented and meaningless. Effective communication relies on shared understanding and agreed-upon meanings for words and phrases.

Conclusion

The impact of non-binary gender on language and communication is significant. It introduces confusion, erodes the richness of our language, and opens the door to a slippery slope where any word or phrase can be questioned and changed. It is important to critically examine the implications of non-binary gender on language and communication, and to consider the long-term consequences of these changes.

While it is important to respect individuals' identities and experiences, we must also recognize the importance of effective communication and shared understanding. Maintaining a binary understanding of gender allows for clear and concise communication, while also respecting the cultural heritage embedded in our language.

Chapter 17: The Legal and Policy Challenges Surrounding Non-Binary Gender Recognition

Introduction

In this chapter, we will explore the legal and policy challenges that arise from the recognition of non-binary gender. While proponents of non-binary gender argue for inclusivity and acceptance, it is essential to critically examine the implications of such recognition. By debunking the myth of non-binary gender, we can better understand the potential pitfalls and problems that arise when attempting to incorporate it into legal frameworks and policies.

The Binary Foundation of Legal Systems

Legal systems around the world are built upon a binary understanding of gender. This binary framework has been in place for centuries and has served as the foundation for various legal rights and responsibilities. Recognizing non-binary gender would require a significant overhaul of these systems, leading to confusion and potential legal loopholes.

Challenges in Identification Documents

One of the primary challenges in recognizing non-binary gender lies in identification documents such as passports, driver's licenses, and birth certificates. These documents have traditionally categorized individuals as either male or female, reflecting the binary understanding of gender. Introducing a third category would create logistical difficulties in maintaining accurate records and verifying identities.

Privacy Concerns

Recognizing non-binary gender raises privacy concerns for individuals who do not wish to disclose their gender identity. In a society where personal information is increasingly accessible, providing a third option for gender could inadvertently expose individuals to discrimination or unwanted attention. Maintaining a binary system helps protect individuals' privacy by allowing them to choose whether or not to disclose their gender.

Impact on Gender-Based Protections

Gender-based protections, such as affirmative action programs and laws against gender discrimination, are designed to address historical inequalities between men and women. Recognizing non-binary gender would complicate these protections, as it blurs the lines between male and female. This could lead to unintended consequences, such as diluting the effectiveness of these measures or creating new forms of discrimination.

Legal Precedents and Precedence

The legal system relies heavily on precedents and established norms. Recognizing non-binary gender would require reevaluating numerous legal precedents that are based on the binary understanding of gender. This process would be time-consuming, costly, and potentially disruptive to the legal system as a whole.

Practical Implementation Challenges

Implementing non-binary gender recognition in practical terms presents numerous challenges. For example, how would institutions such as schools, prisons, and healthcare facilities accommodate individuals who identify as non-binary? The existing infrastructure is not designed to handle such complexities, leading to potential logistical and administrative difficulties.

The Slippery Slope Argument

Recognizing non-binary gender opens the door to an endless array of self-identified genders. If society accepts that individuals can identify outside of the binary, where do we draw the line? This slippery slope argument highlights the potential for chaos and confusion if we abandon the binary understanding of gender altogether.

Conclusion

While proponents of non-binary gender recognition argue for inclusivity and acceptance, it is crucial to critically examine the legal and policy challenges that arise from such recognition. The binary framework has served as the foundation for legal systems for centuries, and deviating from it would create significant logistical, privacy, and implementation challenges. By debunking the myth of non-binary gender, we can better understand the potential pitfalls and problems associated with its recognition.

Chapter 18: Debunking the Notion of a Spectrum between Male and Female

Introduction

In this chapter, we will delve into the fallacy of the notion that there exists a spectrum between male and female. This concept, often used to support the idea of non-binary gender, is deeply flawed and lacks any scientific basis. By examining the biological, psychological, and sociocultural aspects of gender, we will debunk this myth and expose the problem with the belief in a spectrum.

The Biological Reality of Binary Sex

Biologically speaking, humans are a sexually dimorphic species. This means that our species can be categorized into two distinct sexes: male and female. The presence of specific reproductive organs, chromosomes, and hormonal profiles determines an individual's sex. There is no scientific evidence to support the existence of a third or intermediate sex on a biological level.

While some individuals may be born with intersex conditions, these cases are considered medical anomalies rather than evidence for a non-binary gender spectrum. Intersex conditions do not negate the binary nature of sex but rather represent variations within the established male-female framework.

The Psychological Fallacy of Non-Binary Gender

Psychologically, the belief in a non-binary gender spectrum is based on subjective experiences and personal identity rather than empirical evidence. Gender identity is often conflated with gender expression or societal expectations, leading to confusion and misconceptions.

Research consistently shows that the vast majority of individuals identify as either male or female. The existence of transgender individuals who transition from one binary gender to another does not validate the concept of non-binary gender. These individuals still adhere to the binary framework by identifying as either male or female.

Sociocultural Influences on Gender

Sociocultural factors play a significant role in shaping our understanding of gender. However, this does not support the existence of a spectrum between male and female. Societies have historically recognized and categorized individuals into binary genders, with specific roles, expectations, and norms associated with each.

While societal attitudes towards gender have evolved over time, this does not imply the existence of a non-binary gender spectrum. Rather, it reflects a broader acceptance and understanding of transgender individuals who identify as either male or female.

The Problem with Non-Binary Gender

Believing in a non-binary gender spectrum undermines the experiences of individuals who identify as male or female. It dismisses the significance of their identities and perpetuates the notion that gender is a social construct rather than an inherent aspect of our being.

Furthermore, promoting the idea of a non-binary gender spectrum can lead to confusion and distress for individuals who may question their own identity. It creates an environment where self-doubt and uncertainty are encouraged rather than providing clarity and support.

Conclusion

The notion of a spectrum between male and female is a fallacy that lacks scientific evidence and undermines the binary nature of sex. Biological, psychological, and sociocultural factors all point towards the existence of two distinct genders: male and female. Believing in a non-binary gender spectrum only serves to confuse and invalidate the experiences of individuals who identify within the established binary framework.

Chapter 19: Critiquing the Concept of Fluidity in Gender Identity

In this chapter, we will delve into the concept of fluidity in gender identity and critically examine its validity. The idea of gender fluidity suggests that an individual's gender identity can change over time, fluctuating between male, female, or non-binary. However, I argue that this notion is deeply flawed and lacks empirical evidence.

The Fallacy of Gender Fluidity

The concept of gender fluidity rests on the assumption that gender is a social construct and therefore can be fluid and changeable. However, this assumption fails to acknowledge the biological and psychological factors that contribute to an individual's gender identity.

Biologically, individuals are born with either male or female reproductive systems, which determine their sex. This binary distinction forms the basis for the development of gender identity. While there may be rare cases of intersex individuals who possess both male and female biological characteristics, these cases do not negate the existence of a binary system.

Psychologically, research has consistently shown that individuals develop a sense of gender identity early in life. This sense of self is deeply ingrained and stable, with most individuals identifying as either male or female. The idea that one's gender identity can fluctuate undermines the stability and authenticity of one's self-perception.

Lack of Empirical Evidence

Proponents of gender fluidity often argue that personal experiences and anecdotes validate the existence of fluid gender identities. However, personal experiences alone cannot serve as sufficient evidence to support such a significant claim.

To establish the validity of a concept like gender fluidity, empirical evidence is necessary. Yet, studies examining the phenomenon have been limited in scope and plagued by methodological issues. The lack of rigorous scientific research undermines the credibility of gender fluidity as a legitimate concept.

Furthermore, the few studies that have been conducted on gender fluidity have yielded inconsistent and contradictory results. Some suggest that individuals who identify as gender fluid experience changes in their gender identity over time, while others find no evidence to support this claim. Without a clear consensus among researchers, it is premature to accept gender fluidity as a valid concept.

The Danger of Reinforcing Gender Stereotypes

Advocates for gender fluidity argue that it allows individuals to break free from traditional gender norms and expectations. However, this argument fails to recognize the potential harm that can arise from reinforcing stereotypes.

By promoting the idea that one's gender identity can change, we inadvertently reinforce the notion that certain behaviors, interests, and characteristics are inherently tied to specific genders. This perpetuates harmful sterectypes and restricts individuals' freedom to express themselves authentically.

Furthermore, the concept of gender fluidity can undermine the progress made in dismantling gender-based discrimination and inequality. By suggesting that gender is a choice or a fluctuating state, we risk diluting the importance of addressing systemic issues related to gender inequality.

Conclusion

In conclusion, the concept of fluidity in gender identity is deeply flawed and lacks empirical evidence. It fails to acknowledge the biological and psychological factors that contribute to an individual's sense of self. Moreover, promoting the idea of fluid gender identities can reinforce harmful stereotypes and undermine efforts towards achieving true equality.

It is crucial to critically examine and challenge prevailing narratives surrounding non-binary gender identities. By doing so, we can foster a more nuanced understanding of gender and work towards a society that embraces diversity without compromising the integrity of individual identities.

Chapter 20: Understanding the Psychological Implications for Individuals Identifying as Non-Binary

Introduction

In this chapter, we will delve into the psychological implications for individuals who identify as non-binary. While society may be quick to accept and validate non-binary gender identities, it is essential to critically examine the potential harm and fallacies associated with this concept. By understanding the psychological implications, we can better comprehend the underlying issues and challenges faced by those who identify as non-binary.

The Fallacy of Non-Binary Gender

Before delving into the psychological implications, it is crucial to reiterate that non-binary gender is a fallacy. Gender is a binary concept rooted in biological differences between males and females. Non-binary gender attempts to undermine this fundamental truth by suggesting that individuals can exist outside of these categories. However, there is no scientific evidence to support the existence of non-binary gender.

Identity Confusion

One of the primary psychological implications for individuals identifying as non-binary is identity confusion. By rejecting the binary nature of gender, these individuals are left without a clear understanding of their own identity. This confusion can lead to feelings of insecurity, anxiety, and a lack of self-acceptance.

Mental Health Challenges

The rejection of binary gender can also contribute to mental health challenges among those identifying as non-binary. Society's insistence on accepting and validating non-binary identities may inadvertently reinforce the idea that there is something inherently wrong with identifying as male or female. This constant questioning and invalidation can lead to increased rates of depression, anxiety, and other mental health disorders.

Social Isolation

Individuals identifying as non-binary often face social isolation due to their rejection of traditional gender norms. While society may claim to be accepting, the reality is that non-binary individuals are often misunderstood and marginalized. This isolation can lead to feelings of loneliness, alienation, and a lack of support.

Invalidation of Biological Reality

Another psychological implication for individuals identifying as non-binary is the invalidation of biological reality. By rejecting the binary nature of gender, these individuals are essentially denying the biological differences between males and females. This denial can lead to a disconnect from one's own body and a disregard for the importance of biological sex in understanding human beings.

Impact on Relationships

Identifying as non-binary can also have significant implications for personal relationships. The rejection of binary gender can create confusion and uncertainty in romantic partnerships, friendships, and family dynamics. It can be challenging for others to understand and navigate these non-traditional identities, leading to strained relationships and a lack of support.

The Need for Critical Examination

Understanding the psychological implications for individuals identifying as non-binary is crucial in order to have an honest and informed conversation about gender identity. While society may be quick to accept and validate non-binary identities, it is essential to critically examine the potential harm and fallacies associated with this concept. By doing so, we can better support individuals in their journey towards self-acceptance and mental well-being.

Conclusion

In conclusion, the psychological implications for individuals identifying as non-binary are significant. Identity confusion, mental health challenges, social isolation, invalidation of biological reality, and impact on relationships are just a few of the issues faced by those who reject the binary nature of gender. It is essential to critically examine these implications and have an open dialogue about the fallacy of non-binary gender in order to better support individuals in their journey towards self-acceptance and well-being.

Chapter 21: The Role of Parental Influence on Children's Gender Identity

Introduction

In this chapter, we will explore the role of parental influence on children's gender identity. It is crucial to understand how parents can unintentionally contribute to the development of non-binary gender identities in their children. By debunking the myth of non-binary gender, we can shed light on the problematic nature of gender identity and its potential negative impact on children.

The Power of Socialization

Parents play a significant role in socializing their children and shaping their understanding of the world. From an early age, children look to their parents for guidance and validation. Unfortunately, some parents may unknowingly reinforce non-binary gender identities by promoting the idea that gender is fluid and can be chosen at will.

Reinforcing Gender Stereotypes

Parents often inadvertently reinforce gender stereotypes, which can lead to confusion and a distorted understanding of gender identity. By adhering to traditional gender roles and expectations, parents inadvertently contribute to the development of non-binary gender identities in their children.

Parental Acceptance and Validation

Parents who unquestioningly accept and validate their child's non-binary gender identity may inadvertently perpetuate a fallacy. By affirming non-binary gender as a valid concept, parents fail to provide their children with a clear understanding of biological sex and its significance.

The Influence of Media and Peer Pressure

Parents must also consider the influence of media and peer pressure on their child's understanding of gender identity. By exposing children to media that promotes non-binary gender as a valid option, parents indirectly contribute to the development of non-binary gender identities.

Encouraging Critical Thinking

Parents should encourage critical thinking and open dialogue with their children regarding gender identity. By fostering an environment where children can question and explore different perspectives, parents can help their children develop a more nuanced understanding of gender.

Providing a Stable Foundation

Parents must provide a stable foundation for their children's understanding of gender. By emphasizing the importance of biological sex and the inherent differences between males and females, parents can counteract the fallacy of non-binary gender.

Conclusion

In conclusion, parental influence plays a significant role in shaping children's understanding of gender identity. By debunking the myth of non-binary gender and providing a clear understanding of biological sex, parents can help their children develop a more accurate perception of gender. It is essential to recognize the potential negative impact that non-binary gender identities can have on children and work towards promoting a more grounded understanding of gender.

Chapter 22: The Impact of Non-Binary Gender Identity on Relationships and Intimacy

In this chapter, we will explore the detrimental effects of non-binary gender identity on relationships and intimacy. While proponents of non-binary gender may argue that it promotes inclusivity and understanding, the reality is that it creates confusion and undermines the foundations of healthy relationships.

The Illusion of Non-Binary Gender

Non-binary gender is based on the flawed premise that individuals can exist outside the traditional binary understanding of male and female. However, this notion ignores the biological and psychological differences between the sexes, which have evolved over millions of years.

By embracing non-binary gender, individuals are essentially denying their own biology and attempting to redefine themselves based on subjective feelings rather than objective reality. This denial of biological truth can lead to a disconnect between partners in a relationship, as one person may struggle to understand or relate to their non-binary partner's self-perception.

Confusion and Miscommunication

Non-binary gender introduces an additional layer of complexity to relationships, making communication and understanding more challenging. In a traditional relationship, partners can rely on societal norms and expectations to guide their interactions. However, when one partner identifies as non-binary, these norms no longer apply.

For example, in a heterosexual relationship, there are generally understood roles and expectations for each partner based on their biological sex. These roles provide a framework for communication and decision-making. In a non-binary relationship, these roles become blurred or nonexistent, leading to confusion and miscommunication.

Undermining Trust and Stability

Non-binary gender identity can also undermine trust and stability within a relationship. When one partner identifies as non-binary, it introduces uncertainty and unpredictability into the dynamic. The other partner may struggle to understand or anticipate their non-binary partner's needs and desires.

This lack of predictability can erode trust over time, as the non-binary partner's changing identity and preferences may leave their partner feeling insecure or unsure of how to support them. Additionally, the constant questioning of one's own identity and the pressure to conform to a non-binary partner's expectations can lead to emotional strain and resentment.

The Fallacy of Fluidity

Non-binary gender often promotes the idea of fluidity, suggesting that an individual's gender identity can change over time. While proponents argue that this fluidity allows for personal growth and self-discovery, it can also create instability within relationships.

In a traditional relationship, partners can rely on a stable understanding of each other's gender identity. This stability provides a sense of security and allows for the development of deep emotional connections. In contrast, non-binary gender introduces an element of uncertainty, as partners may never know when their non-binary partner's identity will shift.

Conclusion

Non-binary gender identity has a detrimental impact on relationships and intimacy. By denying biological reality and embracing subjective feelings, individuals who identify as non-binary create confusion, miscommunication, and instability within their relationships.

Rather than promoting inclusivity and understanding, non-binary gender undermines the foundations of healthy relationships by eroding trust, introducing unpredictability, and challenging traditional roles and expectations.

It is essential to recognize that non-binary gender is a fallacy that ultimately hinders the development of deep and meaningful connections between partners. By embracing the truth of our biological differences, we can foster healthier and more fulfilling relationships.

Chapter 23: The Challenges Faced by Non-Binary Individuals in the Workplace

Introduction

In this chapter, we will explore the challenges faced by non-binary individuals in the workplace. While proponents of non-binary gender argue for its recognition and acceptance, it is important to critically examine the practical implications of such a concept. By delving into the experiences of non-binary individuals in professional settings, we can better understand the fallacy of non-binary gender and its potential negative impact on individuals and organizations.

The Lack of Legal Protections

One of the significant challenges faced by non-binary individuals in the workplace is the lack of legal protections. Unlike binary genders, which are recognized and protected under existing laws, non-binary gender remains a subjective and ill-defined concept. This lack of legal recognition leaves non-binary individuals vulnerable to discrimination and mistreatment without any recourse.

Confusion and Disruption in Organizational Structures

Non-binary gender poses a significant challenge to organizational structures. Traditional workplaces are built upon a binary understanding of gender, with policies, procedures, and facilities designed to accommodate male and female employees. Introducing non-binary gender into this framework creates confusion and disrupts established norms.

For example, determining appropriate restroom facilities becomes a complex issue. Should organizations be expected to provide separate restrooms for every possible gender identity? This not only creates logistical challenges but also diverts resources away from more pressing matters.

Impact on Team Dynamics

The presence of non-binary individuals in the workplace can also have an adverse impact on team dynamics. Traditional gender roles often play a role in shaping team dynamics, with distinct communication styles and expectations associated with male and female employees.

Introducing non-binary gender challenges these established dynamics, potentially leading to confusion and conflict within teams. This can hinder productivity and collaboration, ultimately affecting the overall success of the organization.

Increased Administrative Burden

Recognizing and accommodating non-binary gender in the workplace also places an increased administrative burden on organizations. Human resources departments must navigate the complexities of gender identity, updating records, policies, and procedures to reflect this new paradigm.

This administrative burden not only consumes valuable time and resources but also detracts from the core functions of HR departments, such as recruitment, training, and employee development.

Conclusion

The challenges faced by non-binary individuals in the workplace highlight the fallacy of non-binary gender. From legal protections to organizational structures and team dynamics, the practical implications of recognizing non-binary gender are fraught with difficulties.

While it is important to foster inclusivity and respect for all individuals, it is equally important to critically examine concepts that lack a solid foundation. Non-binary gender, with its inherent challenges and potential negative impact on organizations, is one such concept that should be debunked rather than embraced.

Chapter 24: The Dangers of Non-Binary Gender Identity in Education and Schools

Introduction

In this chapter, we will explore the dangers of non-binary gender identity in education and schools. We will examine how the acceptance and promotion of non-binary gender can have negative consequences for students, teachers, and the educational system as a whole. By debunking the myth of non-binary gender, we can better understand the potential harm it poses in an educational setting.

1. Undermining Traditional Gender Roles

One of the dangers of non-binary gender identity in education is its potential to undermine traditional gender roles. By promoting the idea that gender is not binary, schools risk confusing students and eroding the foundations of societal norms. Traditional gender roles have been established for centuries and provide a sense of stability and structure in our society. Introducing non-binary gender identity challenges these roles and can lead to confusion and uncertainty among students.

2. Disrupting Classroom Dynamics

Non-binary gender identity can also disrupt classroom dynamics. Teachers are trained to address students using traditional pronouns based on their biological sex. Introducing non-binary pronouns can create confusion and hinder effective communication between teachers and students. This disruption can negatively impact the learning environment and impede educational progress.

3. Encouraging Identity Confusion

Another danger of non-binary gender identity in education is its potential to encourage identity confusion among students. Adolescence is already a time of self-discovery and uncertainty, and introducing non-binary gender as a valid option can further complicate this process. Students may feel pressured to question their own identities, leading to unnecessary stress and confusion.

4. Diverting Resources

Promoting non-binary gender identity in schools diverts valuable resources away from more pressing educational needs. Instead of focusing on improving academic performance and providing necessary resources for students, schools may be forced to allocate time and funding towards promoting non-binary gender identity. This diversion of resources can hinder the overall quality of education and negatively impact students' learning experiences.

5. Ignoring Biological Reality

Non-binary gender identity ignores the biological reality of human beings. It disregards the fact that humans are inherently born with either male or female reproductive systems. By promoting non-binary gender, schools are perpetuating a false narrative that goes against scientific evidence and biological facts. This denial of reality can have long-term consequences for students' understanding of biology and their ability to critically analyze scientific information.

Conclusion

The dangers of non-binary gender identity in education and schools cannot be ignored. By undermining traditional gender roles, disrupting classroom dynamics, encouraging identity confusion, diverting resources, and ignoring biological reality, non-binary gender identity poses a significant threat to the educational system. It is crucial that we debunk the myth of non-binary gender and prioritize the well-being and educational needs of our students.

Chapter 25: The Problem with Non-Binary Gender Representation in Media and Entertainment

Introduction

In this chapter, we will explore the problematic representation of non-binary gender in media and entertainment. While some may argue that increased visibility is a positive step towards acceptance, we will debunk this myth and highlight the dangers of perpetuating the fallacy of non-binary gender.

The Illusion of Choice

One of the main issues with the representation of non-binary gender in media and entertainment is the illusion of choice it presents. By suggesting that individuals can simply choose to identify outside of the traditional binary, we undermine the biological and psychological foundations of gender. This false narrative not only confuses individuals but also perpetuates the idea that gender is a social construct rather than an inherent aspect of our being.

Reinforcing Stereotypes

Another problem with non-binary gender representation in media and entertainment is its tendency to reinforce stereotypes. Rather than challenging societal norms, these portrayals often rely on exaggerated and clichéd depictions that do more harm than good. By reducing non-binary individuals to caricatures, we fail to recognize their unique experiences and perpetuate harmful stereotypes.

Erasure of Biological Reality

The promotion of non-binary gender in media and entertainment also contributes to the erasure of biological reality. By suggesting that gender is solely a matter of personal identification, we ignore the scientific evidence that supports the existence of two distinct biological sexes. This erasure not only undermines our understanding of human biology but also dismisses the experiences of those who identify with their biological sex.

Undermining Feminism

Non-binary gender representation in media and entertainment also poses a threat to feminism. By blurring the lines between male and female, these portrayals undermine the fight for gender equality. Feminism seeks to challenge and dismantle the oppressive structures that perpetuate gender inequality, but non-binary gender representation only serves to confuse and dilute these efforts.

Exploitation for Profit

Lastly, the representation of non-binary gender in media and entertainment often becomes a tool for profit rather than genuine social progress. Companies and individuals capitalize on the trendiness of non-binary identity, using it as a marketing strategy or a way to gain attention. This exploitation not only trivializes the experiences of non-binary individuals but also perpetuates the notion that gender identity is a choice rather than an inherent aspect of our being.

Conclusion

The problematic representation of non-binary gender in media and entertainment perpetuates harmful myths and stereotypes. By promoting the fallacy of non-binary gender, we undermine the biological and psychological foundations of gender, reinforce harmful stereotypes, erase biological reality, undermine feminism, and exploit individuals for profit. It is crucial that we critically examine these portrayals and work towards a more accurate and inclusive understanding of gender.

Chapter 26: Debunking the Link Between Non-Binary Gender and Gender Dysphoria

In this chapter, we will delve into the fallacy of the link between non-binary gender and gender dysphoria. It is crucial to understand that non-binary gender is a concept that lacks scientific evidence and is based on subjective feelings rather than objective reality. By examining the supposed connection between non-binary gender and gender dysphoria, we can further debunk the myth of non-binary gender.

The Flawed Assumption of Gender Dysphoria

Gender dysphoria is a psychological condition where individuals experience distress due to a perceived mismatch between their assigned sex at birth and their gender identity. However, it is important to note that gender dysphoria does not validate the existence of non-binary gender. Gender dysphoria only pertains to individuals who identify as either male or female but feel their assigned sex does not align with their true gender identity.

Non-binary individuals claim to exist outside the traditional binary understanding of male and female. However, this claim lacks scientific evidence and relies solely on personal feelings and subjective experiences. The assumption that non-binary individuals can experience gender dysphoria is flawed because it presupposes the existence of non-binary gender in the first place.

The Inconsistency of Non-Binary Gender and Gender Dysphoria

Another significant flaw in linking non-binary gender with gender dysphoria is the inconsistency within the non-binary community itself. Non-binary individuals often have varying definitions and understandings of what it means to be non-binary. Some may identify as both male and female, while others may reject any association with either binary category.

This inconsistency raises questions about the validity of non-binary gender as a distinct category. If there is no consensus within the non-binary community about what non-binary gender entails, how can we assert that non-binary individuals can experience gender dysphoria? The lack of a clear and consistent definition undermines the credibility of non-binary gender as a legitimate identity.

The Role of Social and Cultural Influences

It is essential to consider the role of social and cultural influences in the emergence of non-binary gender identities. In recent years, there has been a significant increase in the visibility and acceptance of non-binary identities in mainstream society. This increased visibility may contribute to individuals questioning their own gender identity and seeking a non-binary label.

Furthermore, the concept of non-binary gender aligns with contemporary notions of individualism and self-expression. It allows individuals to reject societal norms and create their own unique identity. However, this does not mean that non-binary gender is based on objective reality or scientific evidence.

The Need for Critical Examination

In conclusion, the link between non-binary gender and gender dysphoria is based on flawed assumptions, inconsistency within the non-binary community, and the influence of social and cultural factors. It is crucial to approach the concept of non-binary gender with skepticism and critical examination.

By critically examining the supposed connection between non-binary gender and gender dysphoria, we can debunk the myth of non-binary gender. It is essential to rely on scientific evidence and objective reality rather than subjective feelings when discussing matters as significant as human identity.

Chapter 27: The Controversy Surrounding Non-Binary Gender in Sports

In this chapter, we will explore the controversial topic of non-binary gender in sports. The inclusion of non-binary individuals in traditional binary gender sports categories has sparked heated debates and raised important questions about fairness and competition. However, we will argue that non-binary gender is a fallacy and should not be recognized in the realm of sports.

The Importance of Binary Gender Categories in Sports

Sports have long been divided into male and female categories based on biological sex. This division is not arbitrary but is rooted in the physiological differences between males and females, which can significantly impact athletic performance. Recognizing these differences allows for fair competition and ensures that athletes compete against others with similar physical attributes.

Non-binary gender challenges this fundamental principle by suggesting that individuals can exist outside the traditional male-female binary. However, without clear guidelines on how to define and categorize non-binary athletes, it becomes impossible to ensure fair competition.

The Problem with Including Non-Binary Athletes

Including non-binary athletes in traditional binary gender sports categories raises several concerns. Firstly, it undermines the purpose of having separate categories based on biological sex. If anyone can identify as non-binary and compete in either category, it erases the distinction between male and female athletes.

Secondly, allowing non-binary individuals to compete in binary gender categories could create an unfair advantage or disadvantage for other athletes. Non-binary individuals may possess physical attributes that fall outside the typical range for males or females, making it difficult to determine which category they should compete in.

Moreover, the inclusion of non-binary athletes could lead to a decline in female participation in sports. If non-binary individuals dominate female sports categories due to their unique physical attributes, it may discourage cisgender females from participating, as they may feel they cannot compete on an equal playing field.

The Need for Clear Guidelines

To address the controversy surrounding non-binary gender in sports, clear guidelines must be established. These guidelines should consider the physiological differences between males and females and provide a fair and inclusive framework for competition.

One possible solution is to create a separate category specifically for non-binary athletes. This would allow them to compete against others who share similar physical attributes and abilities. However, this approach raises questions about the feasibility and practicality of implementing such a category.

Another option is to require non-binary athletes to choose a binary gender category based on their biological sex. While this may not align with their gender identity, it would ensure fair competition by grouping athletes with similar physical attributes together.

Conclusion

The controversy surrounding non-binary gender in sports highlights the need for clear guidelines that prioritize fairness and competition. Non-binary gender is a fallacy that challenges the fundamental principles of binary gender categories in sports. It is essential to recognize the physiological differences between males and females and establish a framework that allows for fair competition while respecting individual identities.

Chapter 28: Analyzing the Role of Non-Binary Gender Identity in Mental Health

In this chapter, we will delve into the role of non-binary gender identity in mental health. While proponents of non-binary gender argue that it is a valid and necessary identity, we will explore the potential negative consequences that can arise from embracing this fallacious concept.

The Dangers of Non-Binary Gender Identity

Non-binary gender identity is built upon the notion that individuals can exist outside of the traditional binary understanding of male and female. However, this belief system can have detrimental effects on an individual's mental health.

1. Identity Confusion

By promoting the idea that gender exists on a spectrum, non-binary gender identity creates confusion and uncertainty in individuals who may already be struggling with their sense of self. The pressure to fit into a specific gender category is replaced with the burden of navigating an infinite number of possibilities.

This constant questioning of one's identity can lead to anxiety, depression, and a lack of stability in one's sense of self. It becomes difficult for individuals to establish a solid foundation for their identity when they are constantly questioning whether they truly belong in any particular gender category.

2. Reinforcing Gender Stereotypes

Non-binary gender identity inadvertently reinforces harmful gender stereotypes by suggesting that certain traits or behaviors are inherently masculine or feminine. By embracing a non-binary identity, individuals may feel pressured to conform to these stereotypes in order to validate their own gender expression.

For example, someone assigned female at birth who identifies as non-binary may feel compelled to adopt traditionally masculine traits or behaviors in order to be seen as valid. This perpetuates the idea that certain traits are inherently tied to one's gender, further limiting individual expression and reinforcing harmful societal norms.

3. Lack of Social Support

Non-binary gender identity is still widely misunderstood and stigmatized in society. This lack of understanding can lead to a lack of social support for individuals who identify as non-binary.

Without a supportive community or network, individuals may feel isolated and rejected, which can have severe negative impacts on their mental health. The constant need to explain and defend one's identity can be emotionally draining and lead to feelings of alienation.

The Need for a Rational Approach

It is crucial to approach the concept of non-binary gender identity with a rational mindset. While it is important to respect individuals' self-identified genders, it is equally important to critically examine the validity and potential consequences of embracing non-binary gender as a societal construct.

By promoting a binary understanding of gender, we can provide individuals with a clear framework for understanding their own identities. This clarity can alleviate the confusion and uncertainty that often accompanies non-binary gender identity.

Furthermore, by challenging the notion that certain traits or behaviors are inherently tied to one's gender, we can create a more inclusive society that allows for greater individual expression and freedom.

Conclusion

Non-binary gender identity may seem like an empowering concept on the surface, but upon closer examination, it becomes clear that it can have detrimental effects on an individual's mental health. The confusion, reinforcement of stereotypes, and lack of social support associated with non-binary gender all contribute to its fallacious nature.

It is essential that we approach the concept of non-binary gender with a critical mindset, recognizing the potential harm it can cause. By promoting a rational understanding of gender, we can create a society that is more inclusive and supportive of all individuals, without perpetuating harmful stereotypes or causing unnecessary confusion.

Chapter 29: The Influence of Social Media on Non-Binary Gender Identity

In recent years, social media has played a significant role in shaping public opinion and influencing various aspects of our lives. One area where its impact is particularly evident is in the realm of gender identity. Social media platforms have become breeding grounds for the promotion and acceptance of non-binary gender identities. However, upon closer examination, it becomes clear that social media's influence on non-binary gender identity is not only misguided but also detrimental to society as a whole.

The Echo Chamber Effect

One of the primary reasons why social media has been so influential in promoting non-binary gender identity is the echo chamber effect. Social media algorithms are designed to show users content that aligns with their existing beliefs and preferences. This means that individuals who already identify as non-binary are more likely to be exposed to content that reinforces their beliefs, while dissenting opinions are filtered out.

This echo chamber effect creates an environment where non-binary gender identity is presented as the norm, leading individuals to believe that it is a widely accepted and valid concept. However, this perception is far from reality. The overwhelming majority of people still adhere to the traditional binary understanding of gender, and social media's influence should not be mistaken for widespread acceptance.

The Dangers of Misinformation

Another concerning aspect of social media's influence on non-binary gender identity is the spread of misinformation. On these platforms, anyone can claim to be an expert on gender identity without any formal training or qualifications. This leads to the proliferation of inaccurate information and pseudoscience.

For example, some proponents of non-binary gender argue that it is a natural and inherent aspect of human biology. However, there is no scientific evidence to support this claim. Biological sex is determined by the presence of specific chromosomes, hormones, and reproductive organs, all of which align with the binary understanding of gender. Non-binary gender identity, on the other hand, is a social construct that lacks a solid foundation in biology.

By spreading misinformation about non-binary gender identity, social media platforms are contributing to the confusion and misunderstanding surrounding this topic. This can have serious consequences for individuals who are questioning their own gender identity or seeking accurate information.

Conclusion

While social media has undoubtedly played a significant role in promoting non-binary gender identity, it is essential to critically examine its influence. The echo chamber effect, spread of misinformation, and reinforcement of harmful stereotypes all contribute to a distorted understanding of non-binary gender.

It is crucial to approach discussions about gender identity with skepticism and rely on evidence-based research rather than social media trends. By doing so, we can debunk the myth of non-binary gender and foster a more informed and inclusive society.

Chapter 30: The Impact of Non-Binary Gender on Body Image and Self-Esteem

Introduction

In this chapter, we will explore the detrimental impact of non-binary gender on body image and self-esteem. While proponents of non-binary gender argue that it provides individuals with a sense of liberation and freedom, we will demonstrate that it actually perpetuates harmful societal expectations and pressures. By debunking the myth of non-binary gender, we can pave the way for a healthier understanding of gender identity.

The Illusion of Choice

Non-binary gender presents itself as an alternative to the traditional binary understanding of male and female. However, this illusion of choice only serves to further confine individuals within rigid societal expectations. By claiming to be neither male nor female, non-binary gender inadvertently reinforces the idea that one must fit into one of these two categories. This pressure to choose between two limited options can lead to feelings of inadequacy and self-doubt.

Unrealistic Beauty Standards

Non-binary gender often promotes a rejection of traditional gender norms, including those related to appearance. However, this rejection does not eliminate the influence of societal beauty standards. In fact, it can exacerbate the pressure to conform to an alternative set of unrealistic expectations. Non-binary individuals may feel compelled to present themselves in a way that aligns with a specific non-binary aesthetic, which can be just as restrictive as traditional gender norms.

The Role of Social Media

Social media platforms have played a significant role in popularizing non-binary gender and shaping its representation. While these platforms claim to provide spaces for self-expression and acceptance, they often perpetuate harmful comparisons and unrealistic standards. Non-binary individuals may feel pressured to curate their online presence to fit a specific non-binary image, leading to feelings of inadequacy and low self-esteem when they are unable to meet these expectations.

The Impact on Mental Health

The pressure to conform to non-binary gender can have a profound impact on an individual's mental health. Constantly striving to fit into a specific non-binary identity can lead to anxiety, depression, and body dysmorphia. The focus on appearance and presentation can overshadow other aspects of an individual's identity, leading to a loss of self-worth and a distorted sense of self.

Reinforcing Gender Stereotypes

Ironically, non-binary gender can reinforce gender stereotypes rather than challenging them. By emphasizing the need for individuals to present themselves in a way that aligns with a specific non-binary identity, it perpetuates the idea that one's appearance and behavior must align with their gender identity. This reinforces the harmful notion that one's gender determines their interests, abilities, and personality traits.

The Importance of Authenticity

Rather than subscribing to the fallacy of non-binary gender, we should encourage individuals to embrace their authentic selves. True liberation comes from accepting and celebrating the diversity of human experiences without confining individuals within rigid categories. By rejecting the myth of non-binary gender, we can create a society that values individuality and self-expression without imposing unrealistic expectations.

Conclusion

Non-binary gender may claim to provide individuals with freedom and liberation, but in reality, it perpetuates harmful societal expectations and pressures. By debunking this myth, we can pave the way for a healthier understanding of gender identity that promotes self-acceptance and authenticity. It is time to challenge the fallacy of non-binary gender and embrace a more inclusive and compassionate approach to gender.

Chapter 31: The Role of Cultural Appropriation in Non-Binary Gender Discourse

In this chapter, we will explore the role of cultural appropriation in non-binary gender discourse. Cultural appropriation refers to the adoption or use of elements from another culture without understanding or respecting its original meaning and significance. It is a phenomenon that has gained significant attention in recent years, particularly in discussions surrounding race and ethnicity. However, cultural appropriation also plays a significant role in the discourse surrounding non-binary gender.

Non-binary gender is often presented as a progressive and inclusive concept that challenges traditional notions of male and female. Advocates argue that it allows individuals to express their unique identities outside of the binary framework. However, upon closer examination, it becomes clear that non-binary gender is deeply rooted in cultural appropriation.

The Erasure of Indigenous Cultures

One of the main ways in which cultural appropriation manifests in non-binary gender discourse is through the erasure of indigenous cultures. Non-binary gender is often presented as a universal concept that transcends cultural boundaries. However, this erases the fact that many indigenous cultures have long recognized and respected non-binary identities.

For example, many Native American tribes have historically recognized Two-Spirit individuals who embody both masculine and feminine qualities. These individuals hold sacred roles within their communities and are seen as having a unique spiritual connection. By appropriating and universalizing non-binary gender, proponents of this concept erase the rich history and cultural significance of Two-Spirit identities.

The Commodification of Gender

Another way in which cultural appropriation manifests in non-binary gender discourse is through the commodification of gender. Non-binary gender is often presented as a fashion statement or trend, with individuals adopting certain clothing styles or pronouns to signal their non-binary identity.

This commodification reduces non-binary gender to a mere fashion choice, devoid of its cultural and historical significance. It turns something deeply personal and meaningful for many individuals into a shallow trend that can be easily discarded.

The Exoticization of Non-Western Cultures

Non-binary gender discourse often exoticizes non-Western cultures, particularly those that have long recognized and respected non-binary identities. These cultures are portrayed as mysterious and otherworldly, with their gender practices seen as more enlightened or progressive than Western norms.

This exoticization perpetuates harmful stereotypes and reinforces the idea that non-binary gender is only valid when it is associated with non-Western cultures. It fails to recognize that non-binary identities exist in all cultures, albeit in different forms.

Conclusion

In conclusion, cultural appropriation plays a significant role in non-binary gender discourse. It erases the rich history and cultural significance of non-binary identities in indigenous cultures, commodifies gender as a fashion trend, and exoticizes non-Western cultures. By understanding and addressing these issues, we can have a more nuanced and respectful conversation about gender identity.

Chapter 32: Debunking the Notion of Non-Binary Gender as a Revolutionary Concept

In this chapter, we will delve into the fallacy of non-binary gender as a revolutionary concept. While proponents of non-binary gender argue that it is a groundbreaking and liberating idea, we will demonstrate that it is nothing more than a misguided attempt to reject the biological reality of male and female.

The Biological Basis of Gender

Before we can debunk the notion of non-binary gender, it is crucial to understand the biological basis of gender. From the moment of conception, our bodies are programmed to develop as either male or female. This process is determined by our sex chromosomes, with XX resulting in female development and XY resulting in male development.

The existence of only two sexes is not a social construct but a scientific fact. It is rooted in the fundamental principles of biology and has been observed across countless species throughout history. To deny this reality is to deny the very essence of our existence.

The Problem with Gender Identity

If gender can be self-defined, then what is to stop individuals from identifying as something entirely unrelated to their biology? Should we accept the notion that someone can identify as a different species or even an inanimate object? This has been happening in British schools, with children being allowed to identify as cats, horses and even a moon! The concept of gender identity blurs the line between reality and fantasy, leading to a society untethered from objective truth.

The Impact on Society

Advocates for non-binary gender argue that accepting and validating non-binary identities is essential for creating an inclusive society.

However, this argument fails to consider the broader implications of such a shift.

By rejecting the binary nature of gender, we undermine the foundations of our social structures. Gender roles and expectations have evolved over centuries based on the biological differences between males and females. To disregard these differences is to disregard the unique contributions that each sex brings to society.

Furthermore, by promoting non-binary gender as a valid concept, we risk erasing the experiences of those who identify strongly with their biological sex. It is essential to recognize and celebrate the diversity within the male and female categories without diminishing their significance.

Conclusion

In conclusion, non-binary gender is not a revolutionary concept but a fallacy that disregards the biological basis of gender. By denying the binary nature of male and female, we undermine our understanding of human biology and risk eroding the foundations of our society.

It is crucial to approach discussions about gender with scientific rigor and respect for objective truth. Only by doing so can we foster a society that embraces diversity while acknowledging the fundamental realities of our existence.

Chapter 33: The Problem with Erasing Biological Differences in Non-Binary Gender Discourse

In the ongoing discourse surrounding non-binary gender, one of the most concerning aspects is the erasure of biological differences. Advocates for non-binary gender often argue that gender is a social construct and that biological sex should not be a determining factor in how individuals identify. However, this line of thinking ignores the fundamental reality of biological differences between male and female.

Biological sex is not simply a social construct; it is a scientific fact. From the moment of conception, our bodies develop in distinct ways based on our chromosomal makeup. This leads to the development of primary and secondary sexual characteristics that differentiate males from females. These differences are not arbitrary or socially constructed; they are rooted in biology.

By erasing these biological differences, proponents of non-binary gender are disregarding centuries of scientific research and understanding. They are attempting to redefine what it means to be male or female based solely on individual feelings and subjective experiences.

The Fallacy of Gender Identity

Central to the argument for non-binary gender is the concept of gender identity. Advocates claim that an individual's internal sense of their own gender should be the determining factor in how they are recognized and treated by society. However, this notion is deeply flawed.

Gender identity is a subjective experience that cannot be objectively measured or verified. It is based on personal feelings and perceptions, which can vary greatly from person to person. This subjectivity makes it impossible to establish any concrete criteria for determining someone's gender identity.

Furthermore, by prioritizing gender identity over biological sex, we risk undermining the importance of biology in understanding human beings. Our biological sex has significant implications for our health, reproductive capabilities, and overall well-being. Ignoring these realities in favor of subjective feelings is not only misguided but potentially harmful.

The Danger of Erasing Biological Differences

Erasing biological differences in non-binary gender discourse has serious consequences. By denying the importance of biology, we undermine the scientific understanding of human beings and perpetuate a false narrative that gender is entirely divorced from our physical bodies.

This erasure also dismisses the experiences of individuals who have struggled with their biological sex and have undergone medical interventions, such as hormone therapy or surgery, to align their bodies with their gender identity. By suggesting that biological sex is irrelevant, we invalidate the very real challenges these individuals have faced and the choices they have made to live authentically.

Additionally, erasing biological differences can have unintended consequences for marginalized communities. Women, for example, have historically faced discrimination and oppression based on their biological sex. By erasing this distinction, we risk diluting the fight for women's rights and undermining efforts to address systemic inequalities.

Conclusion

The erasure of biological differences in non-binary gender discourse is a fallacy that ignores scientific reality and undermines the importance of biology in understanding human beings. By prioritizing subjective feelings over objective facts, we risk perpetuating harmful narratives and undermining efforts to address systemic inequalities.

It is crucial that we recognize and respect the biological differences between male and female while also acknowledging the complexity of gender identity. Only by embracing both aspects can we foster a more inclusive and nuanced understanding of gender that respects the diversity of human experiences without erasing the fundamental realities of biology.

Chapter 34: Critiquing the Medical Transition Process for Non-Binary Individuals

In this chapter, we will examine the medical transition process for non-binary individuals and critique its validity. We will argue that this process is based on flawed assumptions and lacks scientific evidence to support its effectiveness.

The Fallacy of Non-Binary Gender

Before delving into the critique of the medical transition process, it is important to reiterate the fallacy of non-binary gender itself. Non-binary gender posits that individuals can exist outside of the traditional binary categories of male and female. However, this concept is not grounded in biological reality.

Biological sex is determined by the presence of either XX or XY chromosomes, which leads to the development of male or female reproductive systems. There is no scientific evidence to support the existence of a third or non-binary sex category. Therefore, any claims of non-binary gender are purely subjective and lack a basis in objective reality.

The Lack of Scientific Evidence

The medical transition process for non-binary individuals relies heavily on hormone therapy and surgeries to align their physical appearance with their self-identified gender. However, there is a lack of scientific evidence to support the effectiveness and long-term outcomes of these interventions for non-binary individuals.

Studies on hormone therapy and surgeries have primarily focused on binary transgender individuals, who identify as either male or female. The limited research available suggests that these interventions can alleviate gender dysphoria in binary transgender individuals. However, extrapolating these findings to non-binary individuals is scientifically unfounded.

Non-binary individuals do not fit neatly into the male or female categories, making it difficult to determine the appropriate hormonal and surgical interventions for them. Without a clear understanding of how these interventions may affect non-binary individuals, it is irresponsible to subject them to potentially irreversible medical procedures.

The Ethical Concerns

Beyond the lack of scientific evidence, there are also ethical concerns surrounding the medical transition process for non-binary individuals. The medical community has a responsibility to prioritize patient well-being and ensure that interventions are based on sound scientific principles.

By offering hormone therapy and surgeries to non-binary individuals without sufficient evidence, the medical community risks exposing them to unnecessary physical and psychological harm. These interventions can have serious side effects and complications, which may outweigh any potential benefits.

Furthermore, the medical transition process may reinforce the fallacy of non-binary gender by legitimizing it as a valid identity. This can perpetuate confusion and undermine the understanding of biological sex as a fundamental aspect of human existence.

Conclusion

In conclusion, the medical transition process for non-binary individuals is based on flawed assumptions and lacks scientific evidence to support its effectiveness. Non-binary gender itself is a fallacy that does not align with biological reality.

The medical community should prioritize evidence-based interventions that prioritize patient well-being and avoid subjecting non-binary individuals to potentially irreversible procedures without sufficient scientific understanding. It is crucial to critically examine and challenge the prevailing narrative surrounding non-binary gender in order to promote a more accurate understanding of human biology and identity.

Chapter 35: Understanding the Societal Pressure to Identify as Non-Binary

Introduction

In this chapter, we will explore the societal pressure that exists to identify as non-binary. Despite the lack of scientific evidence supporting the existence of non-binary gender, society has embraced this concept and created an environment where individuals feel compelled to identify outside of the traditional binary genders. We will examine the various factors that contribute to this pressure and shed light on the fallacy of non-binary gender.

Social Media Influence

One of the primary sources of societal pressure to identify as non-binary is social media. Platforms like Instagram, Twitter, and TikTok have become breeding grounds for promoting non-binary identities as trendy and progressive. Influencers and celebrities often use their platforms to advocate for non-binary gender, creating a sense of desirability around this identity.

However, it is crucial to recognize that social media is not a reliable source of information or scientific evidence. The pressure to conform to non-binary gender norms on these platforms is based on popularity rather than factual accuracy. Individuals may feel compelled to identify as non-binary simply because it is seen as fashionable or socially acceptable.

Peer Influence

Another significant factor contributing to the societal pressure to identify as non-binary is peer influence. In many social circles, particularly among younger generations, there is a strong emphasis on inclusivity and acceptance of diverse gender identities.

While it is essential to create an inclusive environment for all individuals, it is equally important not to confuse inclusivity with scientific validity. Peer pressure can lead individuals to question their own gender identity and feel compelled to identify as non-binary, even if it does not align with their true feelings or experiences.

Misunderstanding of Gender

The societal pressure to identify as non-binary is also fueled by a widespread misunderstanding of gender. Many people mistakenly believe that gender is solely a social construct and that individuals can choose their gender identity based on personal preference.

However, scientific research consistently demonstrates that gender is a complex interplay of biological, psychological, and social factors. It is not a matter of personal choice or societal pressure. By perpetuating the myth of non-binary gender, society fails to acknowledge the biological and psychological realities that underpin gender identity.

Political Correctness

The pressure to identify as non-binary is further exacerbated by the prevailing culture of political correctness. In an effort to be inclusive and avoid offending anyone, individuals may feel compelled to adopt non-binary gender identities or support those who do.

However, it is crucial to distinguish between genuine inclusivity and the uncritical acceptance of fallacious concepts. By blindly embracing non-binary gender without questioning its validity, society risks undermining the scientific understanding of gender and perpetuating harmful misconceptions.

Conclusion

The societal pressure to identify as non-binary is a result of various factors, including social media influence, peer pressure, misunderstanding of gender, and political correctness. However, it is essential to critically examine these influences and recognize the fallacy of non-binary gender.

By promoting a more nuanced understanding of gender that acknowledges its biological and psychological foundations, we can move away from the societal pressure to conform to non-binary identities and foster a more accurate and inclusive understanding of human diversity.

Chapter 36: Debunking the Argument for Legal Recognition of Non-Binary Gender

In this chapter, we will examine the argument for legal recognition of non-binary gender and debunk its fallacies. Non-binary gender is a concept that asserts the existence of genders beyond the traditional binary of male and female. Advocates argue that legal recognition is necessary to protect the rights and identities of individuals who do not identify as strictly male or female. However, upon closer examination, it becomes clear that this argument is deeply flawed.

1. Lack of Scientific Evidence

The first and most significant flaw in the argument for legal recognition of non-binary gender is the lack of scientific evidence supporting its existence. Gender identity is a complex topic that has been extensively studied by psychologists, biologists, and neuroscientists. Yet, there is no consensus among experts regarding the existence of non-binary gender.

Advocates often rely on personal anecdotes and subjective experiences to support their claims. While these stories are undoubtedly important, they do not constitute scientific evidence. Without empirical data and rigorous research, it is impossible to establish non-binary gender as a valid and distinct category.

2. Slippery Slope Argument

Another fallacy in the argument for legal recognition of non-binary gender is the slippery slope it creates. If we accept non-binary gender as a valid category, where do we draw the line? If individuals can identify as neither male nor female, what prevents others from identifying as animals or objects?

By opening the door to limitless self-identification, we undermine the very concept of gender itself. Gender becomes a subjective construct detached from biological reality, leading to confusion and chaos in legal systems that rely on clear definitions.

3. Legal Implications

Legal recognition of non-binary gender would have far-reaching implications for society. It would require significant changes to existing laws, documents, and systems that are based on the binary understanding of gender. This would create unnecessary administrative burdens and confusion.

Furthermore, legal recognition of non-binary gender could undermine the rights and protections currently afforded to women and men. Gender-based policies and affirmative action programs aimed at addressing historical inequalities may become obsolete or ineffective if gender loses its clear definition.

4. Inconsistencies in Non-Binary Gender

Non-binary gender is inherently inconsistent and self-contradictory. Advocates argue that gender is a social construct, yet they also claim that non-binary gender is an innate identity. This contradiction undermines the credibility of the argument for legal recognition.

Additionally, non-binary gender encompasses a wide range of identities, from agender to bigender to genderfluid. These identities often have conflicting definitions and experiences, further complicating the notion of legal recognition.

5. Alternative Solutions

Lastly, it is important to consider alternative solutions to address the concerns raised by advocates of non-binary gender. Rather than pushing for legal recognition, we should focus on creating inclusive environments that respect individuals' self-identified genders without erasing the biological reality of male and female.

This can be achieved through education, awareness campaigns, and workplace policies that promote diversity and inclusion. By fostering understanding and acceptance, we can create a society that respects individual identities without compromising the integrity of established legal frameworks.

Conclusion

In conclusion, the argument for legal recognition of non-binary gender is deeply flawed. It lacks scientific evidence, creates a slippery slope, has significant legal implications, is inconsistent, and ignores alternative solutions. While it is important to respect individuals' identities, we must also critically examine the validity and practicality of concepts such as non-binary gender. Only through rigorous analysis can we ensure that our legal systems remain fair, just, and grounded in reality.

Chapter 37: The Role of Religion and Spirituality in Challenging Non-Binary Gender Identity

Introduction

In this chapter, I explore the role of religion and spirituality in challenging the concept of non-binary gender identity. While some may argue that religion and spirituality have no place in discussions about gender, it is important to recognize the significant influence these belief systems have on shaping societal norms and values. By examining religious teachings and spiritual perspectives, we can gain a deeper understanding of why non-binary gender is a fallacy.

Religious Teachings on Gender

Many major religions have specific teachings on gender that emphasize a binary understanding of male and female. For example, in Christianity, the Bible states that God created humans male and female (Genesis 1:27). This binary view is further reinforced by passages that discuss marriage as being between a man and a woman (Matthew 19:4-6). Similarly, Islam teaches that Allah created humans as either male or female, with distinct roles and responsibilities assigned to each gender.

These religious teachings provide a clear framework for understanding gender as a binary concept. Non-binary gender identity contradicts these teachings by suggesting that individuals can exist outside of the traditional male-female dichotomy. By challenging the binary understanding of gender, non-binary identities undermine the religious foundations upon which many societies are built.

Spiritual Perspectives on Gender

Beyond organized religion, spirituality often plays a significant role in shaping individuals' beliefs about gender. Many spiritual traditions emphasize the importance of balance and harmony between masculine and feminine energies. However, this does not imply the existence of non-binary gender identities.

Spiritual perspectives often view masculine and feminine energies as complementary rather than separate entities. The concept of yin and yang in Taoism, for example, represents the interplay between opposing but interconnected forces. This understanding does not support the idea that individuals can exist outside of the binary framework.

Furthermore, spiritual practices often involve rituals and ceremonies that reinforce traditional gender roles. For instance, in many indigenous cultures, gender-specific rituals are performed to mark important life transitions. These rituals reaffirm the binary understanding of gender and reinforce the idea that non-binary identities are not valid.

The Fallacy of Non-Binary Gender

Religious teachings and spiritual perspectives provide a strong foundation for debunking the myth of non-binary gender identity. By emphasizing a binary understanding of gender and reinforcing traditional gender roles, these belief systems challenge the validity of non-binary identities.

Non-binary gender is a fallacy because it contradicts deeply ingrained religious and spiritual beliefs that have shaped societies for centuries. It undermines the stability and coherence of these belief systems by suggesting that there are more than two genders.

Conclusion

Religion and spirituality play a crucial role in challenging the concept of non-binary gender identity. By examining religious teachings and spiritual perspectives, we can see how these belief systems uphold a binary understanding of gender and reinforce traditional gender roles. Non-binary gender is a fallacy because it contradicts these deeply ingrained beliefs and undermines the stability of religious and spiritual frameworks. It is essential to recognize the influence of religion and spirituality in discussions about gender identity to fully understand why non-binary gender is invalid.

Chapter 38: The Problem with Co-opting Intersex Narratives for Non-Binary Gender Discourse

Introduction

In recent years, there has been a growing trend of co-opting intersex narratives to support the concept of non-binary gender. Advocates argue that intersex individuals, who are born with physical characteristics that do not fit typical definitions of male or female, provide evidence for the existence of non-binary gender identities. However, this chapter will argue that this co-optation is problematic and does not hold up under scrutiny.

The Distinction Between Intersex and Non-Binary Gender

It is important to first establish a clear distinction between intersex individuals and non-binary gender identities. Intersex is a medical condition characterized by atypical physical sex characteristics, such as ambiguous genitalia or variations in chromosomes. Non-binary gender, on the other hand, refers to individuals who do not identify exclusively as male or female.

While both intersex and non-binary individuals challenge traditional notions of binary gender, it is crucial to recognize that they are distinct concepts. Intersex is a biological condition, whereas non-binary gender is a subjective identity.

The Fallacy of Equating Intersex with Non-Binary Gender

Advocates for non-binary gender often argue that the existence of intersex individuals supports the idea that gender exists on a spectrum. They claim that because intersex individuals do not neatly fit into the categories of male or female, it follows that there must be other genders beyond these binary options.

However, this argument is flawed. Intersex conditions are purely biological and do not inherently imply anything about an individual's gender identity. It is important to respect the experiences and identities of intersex individuals without using their narratives to support non-binary gender.

Respecting Intersex Individuals' Autonomy

Co-opting intersex narratives for non-binary gender discourse also raises ethical concerns. Intersex individuals have long been subjected to medical interventions and societal pressures to conform to binary gender norms. By using their experiences to support non-binary gender, we risk further erasing their autonomy and perpetuating harmful practices.

It is crucial to listen to intersex individuals and respect their right to self-identify. We should not impose non-binary gender identities onto them or use their stories as evidence for the validity of such identities.

The Importance of Evidence-Based Arguments

Lastly, it is essential to base our arguments on evidence rather than relying on emotional appeals or co-opting other marginalized groups' narratives. While it is important to acknowledge and support diverse gender identities, we must do so in a way that is grounded in scientific research and respects the autonomy of all individuals involved.

By relying on intersex narratives without solid evidence, we risk undermining the credibility of the non-binary gender movement and reinforcing harmful stereotypes about gender identity.

Conclusion

Co-opting intersex narratives for non-binary gender discourse is problematic and does not withstand scrutiny. Intersex conditions are purely biological, while non-binary gender identities are subjective experiences. It is crucial to respect the autonomy of intersex individuals and base our arguments on evidence rather than emotional appeals. By doing so, we can foster a more inclusive understanding of gender without erasing the unique experiences of intersex individuals.

Chapter 39: Examining the Influence of Postmodernism on Non-Binary Gender Theory

Introduction

In recent years, there has been a surge in the acceptance and promotion of non-binary gender identities. This shift in societal attitudes towards gender has been heavily influenced by postmodernist ideology. Postmodernism, with its rejection of objective truth and embrace of subjectivity, has created an environment where non-binary gender theory can flourish. However, upon closer examination, it becomes clear that the foundations of non-binary gender are built on shaky ground.

The Problem with Postmodernism

Postmodernism is a philosophical framework that rejects the notion of objective truth and instead emphasizes the importance of individual experiences and perspectives. While this may sound appealing in theory, it creates a dangerous precedent when applied to the concept of gender.

By denying the existence of objective truth, postmodernism opens the door for individuals to define their own reality. This leads to a situation where anyone can claim to be non-binary without any objective criteria or evidence to support their claim.

The Fallacy of Gender Identity

Non-binary gender theory rests on the assumption that gender is a social construct and that individuals can choose their own gender identity. However, this belief ignores the biological reality of sex and the role it plays in shaping our identities.

Sex is determined by our chromosomes, reproductive organs, and secondary sexual characteristics. It is an objective fact that cannot be changed or chosen. Gender, on the other hand, is a set of social roles and expectations that are typically associated with one's sex.

While it is true that some individuals may not conform to traditional gender norms, this does not mean that they are non-binary. It simply means that they do not fit neatly into the binary categories of male and female. This does not invalidate the existence of binary gender, but rather highlights the need for a more inclusive understanding of gender expression.

The Influence of Confirmation Bias

Confirmation bias is a cognitive bias that leads individuals to interpret and remember information in a way that confirms their preexisting beliefs. In the case of non-binary gender theory, confirmation bias plays a significant role in perpetuating the myth of non-binary gender.

Those who identify as non-binary often seek out information and experiences that validate their identity, while dismissing or ignoring evidence that contradicts it. This selective attention reinforces their belief in non-binary gender and creates an echo chamber where dissenting voices are silenced.

The Dangers of Non-Binary Gender

While it may seem harmless to embrace non-binary gender identities, there are several potential dangers associated with this ideology.

Firstly, by denying the existence of binary gender, non-binary gender theory erases the experiences and struggles of individuals who identify as male or female. It undermines the progress made in achieving equality for women and perpetuates harmful stereotypes about masculinity and femininity.

Secondly, by promoting the idea that anyone can choose their own gender identity, non-binary gender theory undermines the concept of informed consent. It opens the door for individuals to make irreversible decisions about their bodies and identities without fully understanding the long-term consequences.

Conclusion

Non-binary gender theory, heavily influenced by postmodernism, is built on shaky foundations. By rejecting objective truth and embracing subjectivity, it creates a situation where anyone can claim to be non-binary without any objective criteria or evidence. This undermines the biological reality of sex and the importance of gender as a social construct. It also perpetuates confirmation bias and creates an echo chamber where dissenting voices are silenced. Ultimately, the promotion of non-binary gender poses significant dangers to society and undermines the progress made in achieving equality for women.

Chapter 40: Debunking the Notion of Non-Binary Gender as a Natural State

Introduction

In this chapter, we will delve into the fallacy of non-binary gender as a natural state. We will explore the biological, psychological, and sociological aspects that debunk the notion of non-binary gender. By examining the evidence and dismantling the arguments put forth by proponents of non-binary gender, we will reveal the inherent problems with this concept.

The Biological Perspective

Biologically speaking, humans are a sexually dimorphic species. This means that our species can be classified into two distinct sexes: male and female. The presence of specific reproductive organs and genetic makeup determines an individual's sex. There is no scientific evidence to support the existence of a third or non-binary sex.

Furthermore, the concept of non-binary gender contradicts the fundamental principles of evolution. Evolutionary biology has shaped our species to reproduce through sexual reproduction, which requires two distinct sexes. Non-binary gender undermines this basic biological process and lacks any evolutionary advantage.

The Psychological Perspective

Psychologically, non-binary gender is a construct that lacks empirical evidence. Gender identity is often conflated with gender expression or personality traits, leading to confusion and misinterpretation. While individuals may experience discomfort with societal gender norms, it does not validate the existence of non-binary gender as a natural state.

Moreover, studies have shown that individuals who identify as non-binary often have higher rates of mental health issues such as depression and anxiety. This suggests that non-binary gender may be a result of underlying psychological distress rather than an innate characteristic.

The Sociological Perspective

From a sociological standpoint, non-binary gender is a relatively recent phenomenon that has gained traction in certain social circles. It is important to recognize that societal norms and cultural influences play a significant role in shaping gender identities. Non-binary gender can be seen as a product of these influences rather than a natural state.

Furthermore, the concept of non-binary gender undermines the progress made by the feminist movement. By erasing the distinction between male and female, non-binary gender perpetuates the idea that gender is purely a social construct, disregarding the biological realities that women have fought against for centuries.

Conclusion

In conclusion, non-binary gender is a fallacy that lacks scientific, psychological, and sociological evidence. It contradicts our biological nature as a sexually dimorphic species and undermines the principles of evolution. Psychologically, it may be a result of underlying distress rather than an innate characteristic. Sociologically, it can be seen as a product of societal norms and cultural influences.

It is crucial to critically examine and challenge concepts such as non-binary gender to ensure that we maintain an accurate understanding of human nature. By debunking this myth, we can foster a more informed and inclusive society that respects both biological realities and individual experiences.

Chapter 41: The Impact of Non-Binary Gender Identity on Mental Health Diagnosis and Treatment

Introduction

In this chapter, we will explore the detrimental impact of non-binary gender identity on mental health diagnosis and treatment. We will argue that the concept of non-binary gender is a fallacy that undermines the accuracy and effectiveness of mental health care.

Misdiagnosis and Overdiagnosis

The acceptance of non-binary gender identity has led to an increase in misdiagnosis and overdiagnosis of mental health conditions. Mental health professionals are now expected to validate and affirm individuals' self-identified genders, even if they do not align with biological reality.

This pressure to conform to non-binary gender identities can lead to misdiagnoses of conditions such as gender dysphoria or body dysmorphia. Individuals may mistakenly believe that their distress stems from their assigned sex at birth, when in reality, it may be rooted in other underlying psychological issues.

Furthermore, the overdiagnosis of mental health conditions related to non-binary gender identities can result in unnecessary medical interventions such as hormone therapy or surgeries. These interventions may not address the underlying psychological issues and can have long-term negative consequences for individuals' physical and mental well-being.

Undermining Objective Assessment

The acceptance of non-binary gender identity undermines the objective assessment of mental health. Mental health professionals are now expected to prioritize individuals' self-identified genders over biological sex when diagnosing and treating mental health conditions.

This shift towards subjective self-identification hinders accurate assessment and treatment planning. Mental health professionals must consider biological factors, such as hormonal imbalances or genetic predispositions, when diagnosing and treating mental health conditions. Ignoring these factors in favor of non-binary gender identities can lead to ineffective or inappropriate treatment approaches.

The Role of Social Contagion

Non-binary gender identity is not an innate characteristic but rather a social construct that has gained popularity in recent years. The rise in non-binary gender identities can be attributed, in part, to social contagion, where individuals adopt certain beliefs or behaviors due to social influence.

This social contagion has led to a significant increase in the number of individuals identifying as non-binary without proper evaluation or understanding of their own psychological well-being. This trend further complicates mental health diagnosis and treatment, as individuals may adopt non-binary gender identities without fully considering the potential consequences on their mental health.

Conclusion

Non-binary gender identity undermines the accuracy and effectiveness of mental health diagnosis and treatment. By prioritizing subjective self-identification over objective assessment, mental health professionals risk misdiagnosing and overdiagnosing conditions related to non-binary gender identities.

It is crucial to critically examine the concept of non-binary gender and its impact on mental health care. By doing so, we can ensure that individuals receive appropriate and effective treatment based on objective assessment rather than subjective self-identification.

Chapter 42: The Role of Non-Binary Gender Identity in Political Activism

Introduction

In this chapter, we will explore the role of non-binary gender identity in political activism. While proponents of non-binary gender argue that it is a valid and important aspect of human identity, we will debunk this myth and highlight the problems with embracing non-binary gender as a political tool.

The Political Agenda

Non-binary gender identity has become a central component of the political agenda of certain groups. They argue that recognizing and affirming non-binary gender is necessary for achieving equality and social justice. However, this political agenda is built on flawed premises and misguided assumptions.

Undermining Biological Reality

One of the main problems with non-binary gender as a political tool is that it undermines the biological reality of human beings. By claiming that individuals can exist outside of the binary categories of male and female, proponents of non-binary gender ignore the scientific evidence that clearly demonstrates the biological basis of sex.

Ignoring Psychological Research

Another issue with non-binary gender as a political tool is its disregard for psychological research. The vast majority of individuals identify as either male or female, aligning their gender identity with their biological sex. Non-binary gender advocates dismiss this overwhelming evidence and instead promote an ideology that goes against the natural inclinations of most people.

Creating Division and Polarization

Non-binary gender as a political tool also contributes to division and polarization within society. By promoting the idea that there are infinite genders beyond male and female, proponents of non-binary gender create confusion and conflict. This divisive approach hinders progress towards true equality and social cohesion.

Undermining Women's Rights

One of the most concerning aspects of non-binary gender as a political tool is its potential to undermine women's rights. By erasing the distinction between male and female, non-binary gender advocates risk diluting the gains made by women in their fight for equality. This can have serious consequences for issues such as reproductive rights, workplace discrimination, and violence against women.

Distorting Language and Communication

Non-binary gender as a political tool also distorts language and communication. By introducing an ever-expanding list of gender identities, proponents of non-binary gender complicate everyday interactions and make it difficult for individuals to understand and relate to one another. This linguistic confusion hampers effective communication and can lead to misunderstandings and conflicts.

Conclusion

Non-binary gender as a political tool is deeply flawed and problematic. It undermines biological reality, ignores psychological research, creates division and polarization, undermines women's rights, and distorts language and communication. It is crucial to critically examine the claims made by proponents of non-binary gender and recognize the fallacy behind this concept in the context of political activism.

Chapter 43: Analyzing the Influence of Peer Pressure on Non-Binary Gender Identification

Introduction

In this chapter, we will delve into the influence of peer pressure on the identification of non-binary gender. It is crucial to understand the role that external factors play in shaping an individual's perception of their gender identity. By examining the impact of peer pressure, we can better comprehend the fallacy behind non-binary gender and its lack of validity.

The Power of Social Influence

Human beings are social creatures who are susceptible to the influence of their peers. From a young age, individuals seek acceptance and validation from their social circles. This desire for approval often leads people to conform to societal norms and expectations, including those related to gender.

Non-Binary Gender as a Trend

One cannot ignore the fact that non-binary gender has gained significant popularity in recent years. It has become a trend, with many individuals identifying as non-binary without fully understanding or experiencing the complexities of gender dysphoria. This trendiness can be attributed, in part, to peer pressure.

The Need for Belonging

Peer pressure often stems from the need for belonging. Individuals may feel compelled to identify as non-binary because they perceive it as a way to fit in with a particular group or community. The fear of being ostracized or labeled as outdated can push individuals to adopt non-binary gender identification without genuine introspection.

The Influence of Social Media

Social media platforms have played a significant role in promoting non-binary gender identification. The constant exposure to diverse identities and narratives can create a sense of pressure to conform to these new concepts. The desire for online validation and acceptance further fuels the adoption of non-binary gender as individuals seek to gain social approval.

The Role of Peer Reinforcement

Peer reinforcement is a powerful tool in shaping an individual's perception of their gender identity. When surrounded by peers who identify as non-binary, individuals may feel compelled to follow suit to maintain social harmony. This reinforcement can create a false sense of validation and further perpetuate the fallacy of non-binary gender.

The Lack of Genuine Self-Reflection

Peer pressure often discourages genuine self-reflection and critical thinking. Individuals may adopt non-binary gender identification without thoroughly examining their own experiences and feelings. This lack of introspection undermines the validity of non-binary gender, as it is based on external influences rather than genuine self-discovery.

Conclusion

The influence of peer pressure on non-binary gender identification cannot be ignored. The trendiness and desire for acceptance have led many individuals to adopt this identity without genuine introspection or understanding. By recognizing the role of peer pressure, we can better understand the fallacy behind non-binary gender and its lack of validity.

Chapter 44: Debunking the Notion of Non-Binary Gender as an Inherent Human Right

Introduction

It is essential to critically examine this notion and question whether non-binary gender can truly be considered an inherent human right. In this chapter, we will debunk the idea of non-binary gender as a fundamental human right and highlight the problems with basing one's identity on gender.

It is important to note that gender identity is not synonymous with biological sex. While individuals may experience discomfort or incongruence with their assigned sex at birth, it does not negate the existence of only two biological sexes. Non-binary gender attempts to create a new category that lacks a solid foundation in biology or science.

The Problem with Gender Identity

Relying on subjective feelings as the basis for one's identity opens the door to an infinite number of possible gender identities. If gender identity is considered a protected human right, where do we draw the line? Should individuals be able to identify as animals, objects, or even fictional characters? The concept of gender identity lacks clear boundaries and can lead to a slippery slope of identity claims that are detached from reality.

The Importance of Objective Criteria

Recognizing non-binary gender as an inherent human right would require society to abandon objective criteria for determining sex and gender. This would have far-reaching consequences, particularly in areas such as healthcare, sports, and legal documentation.

For instance, if non-binary gender were recognized as a human right, it would be challenging to establish fair and consistent policies in sports competitions. How would we determine which category non-binary athletes should compete in? Without clear guidelines based on biological sex, the integrity of competitive sports would be compromised.

The Potential for Harm

Advocating for non-binary gender as an inherent human right also raises concerns about potential harm to individuals who may be influenced by societal pressure or personal confusion. Gender dysphoria, a recognized medical condition, is often cited as a reason for supporting non-binary gender identities. However, it is crucial to approach this issue with caution.

Encouraging individuals to identify outside of the traditional male or female categories may lead some vulnerable individuals down a path that ultimately does not align with their well-being. It is essential to prioritize mental health and ensure that individuals receive appropriate support and guidance rather than promoting potentially harmful ideologies.

Conclusion

While proponents argue that non-binary gender should be recognized as an inherent human right, it is clear that this notion is deeply flawed. Non-binary gender lacks a solid foundation in biology and science, and the concept of gender identity itself poses significant problems when it comes to defining clear boundaries.

Rather than advocating for non-binary gender as a human right, we should focus on promoting equality and respect for all individuals, regardless of their biological sex or gender identity. By recognizing the importance of objective criteria and prioritizing mental health, we can create a more inclusive society that respects the realities of biology while supporting individuals in their journey towards self-acceptance.

Chapter 45: The Impact of Non-Binary Gender Identity on Parenting and Family Dynamics

Introduction

In this chapter, we will explore the detrimental impact of non-binary gender identity on parenting and family dynamics. Non-binary gender, with its rejection of the traditional binary understanding of male and female, disrupts the stability and structure that is essential for healthy family relationships. By challenging the very foundation of gender roles and expectations, non-binary gender identity undermines the ability of parents to provide a stable environment for their children.

Destabilizing Parental Roles

Non-binary gender identity destabilizes parental roles by blurring the lines between motherhood and fatherhood. The traditional roles of mothers as nurturers and fathers as providers are based on biological differences and have evolved over centuries to ensure the well-being of children. Non-binary gender identity rejects these roles, leaving children confused about their parents' responsibilities and unable to develop a clear understanding of their own gender identity.

Confusing Children's Gender Identity

Non-binary gender identity confuses children about their own gender identity. By presenting multiple options beyond male or female, non-binary ideology creates uncertainty and doubt in children's minds. This confusion can lead to emotional distress and a lack of self-acceptance as children struggle to fit into societal norms or find a stable sense of self.

Undermining Family Values

Non-binary gender identity undermines traditional family values by challenging the importance of biological ties and genetic inheritance. The concept of non-binary gender suggests that family relationships are not based on biological connections but rather on individual self-identification. This undermines the importance of biological parents in a child's life and weakens the bond between parents and their offspring.

Disrupting Family Stability

Non-binary gender identity disrupts family stability by introducing uncertainty and conflict into the household. When parents embrace non-binary gender identities, it can lead to disagreements and tension within the family unit. This instability can have long-lasting negative effects on children's emotional well-being and their ability to form healthy relationships in the future.

Impeding Parental Guidance

Non-binary gender identity impedes parental guidance by challenging the authority of parents to guide their children's understanding of gender. When parents themselves reject the binary understanding of gender, they are unable to provide clear guidance and support to their children. This lack of guidance can leave children feeling lost and unsupported as they navigate their own gender identity.

Conclusion

Non-binary gender identity has a detrimental impact on parenting and family dynamics. By destabilizing parental roles, confusing children's gender identity, undermining family values, disrupting family stability, and impeding parental guidance, non-binary gender ideology poses a significant threat to the well-being of families. It is essential that we debunk the myth of non-binary gender and reaffirm the importance of traditional binary understandings of male and female for the sake of our children and the stability of our families.

Chapter 46: The Role of Non-Binary Gender Identity in Online Communities and Forums

Introduction

In recent years, the concept of non-binary gender has gained significant attention and acceptance in various online communities and forums. Advocates argue that non-binary individuals do not identify exclusively as male or female, but rather as a combination or absence of both genders. However, it is crucial to critically examine the role of non-binary gender identity in these online spaces and question its validity. This chapter aims to debunk the myth of non-binary gender by highlighting the problematic nature of its presence in online communities and forums.

The Proliferation of Pseudonyms

One of the key issues with non-binary gender identity in online communities is the proliferation of pseudonyms. Non-binary individuals often adopt unique usernames or handles that reflect their self-identified gender. This practice not only perpetuates the fallacy of non-binary gender but also undermines the authenticity and credibility of online interactions.

By using pseudonyms, individuals can easily create multiple online personas, blurring the lines between reality and fiction. This phenomenon raises concerns about the sincerity and genuineness of non-binary identities within these spaces. It becomes challenging to discern whether someone genuinely identifies as non-binary or if they are merely adopting a trendy label for attention-seeking purposes.

The Reinforcement of Stereotypes

Another problematic aspect of non-binary gender identity in online communities is its reinforcement of stereotypes. Advocates often claim that non-binary individuals challenge traditional gender norms and expectations. However, by creating separate categories for non-binary identities, these communities inadvertently reinforce the very stereotypes they claim to oppose.

The existence of non-binary gender implies that there are specific traits or characteristics associated with being neither male nor female. This binary thinking perpetuates the notion that individuals must conform to predefined gender roles and behaviors. Rather than dismantling gender stereotypes, non-binary gender identity inadvertently strengthens them.

The Erosion of Language

Non-binary gender identity in online communities also contributes to the erosion of language. Advocates often introduce new pronouns and linguistic constructs to accommodate non-binary individuals. While proponents argue that this promotes inclusivity, it ultimately leads to confusion and dilution of language.

The English language, like many others, has evolved over centuries to reflect the complexities of human experiences. However, introducing a multitude of pronouns and linguistic constructs for non-binary individuals undermines the clarity and efficiency of communication. It becomes increasingly challenging for individuals to navigate these linguistic minefields, hindering effective communication within online communities.

The Absence of Scientific Evidence

Perhaps the most significant flaw in non-binary gender identity within online communities is the absence of scientific evidence supporting its validity. While advocates may argue that personal experiences validate their identities, it is essential to rely on empirical research and scientific consensus when discussing matters of gender.

To date, no scientific study has conclusively proven the existence or legitimacy of non-binary gender. The lack of empirical evidence raises doubts about the validity of non-binary identities within online communities. Without a solid foundation in scientific research, non-binary gender remains nothing more than a subjective belief system.

Conclusion

The presence of non-binary gender identity in online communities and forums is deeply problematic. The proliferation of pseudonyms, reinforcement of stereotypes, erosion of language, and absence of scientific evidence all contribute to the fallacy of non-binary gender. It is crucial to critically examine and challenge these beliefs to foster a more informed and rational understanding of gender identity.

Chapter 47: The Impact of Non-Binary Gender Identity on Mental Health Research and Treatment

Introduction

In recent years, there has been a growing acceptance and recognition of non-binary gender identities. However, this acceptance has not come without consequences. The rise of non-binary gender identity has had a significant impact on mental health research and treatment. In this chapter, we will explore the negative effects of non-binary gender identity on mental health and argue that it is a fallacy that should not be perpetuated.

The Lack of Scientific Evidence

One of the main problems with non-binary gender identity is the lack of scientific evidence supporting its existence. Despite claims made by proponents of non-binary gender, there is no empirical research that conclusively proves the existence of more than two genders. This lack of evidence undermines the credibility of non-binary gender as a valid identity.

The Role of Social Construction

Non-binary gender identity is largely a product of social construction rather than biological reality. It is influenced by societal norms, cultural beliefs, and personal experiences. By promoting non-binary gender as a legitimate identity, we are perpetuating a social construct that has no basis in biology or science. This can have detrimental effects on individuals' mental health by reinforcing false beliefs about their own identities.

The Impact on Mental Health Research

The acceptance and promotion of non-binary gender identity have had a significant impact on mental health research. Researchers are now pressured to include non-binary gender as a category in their studies, despite the lack of scientific evidence supporting its validity. This inclusion can lead to biased results and inaccurate conclusions about the relationship between gender and mental health.

The Problem with Gender Dysphoria Diagnosis

Non-binary gender identity also poses challenges for the diagnosis and treatment of gender dysphoria. Gender dysphoria is a recognized mental health condition characterized by distress caused by a mismatch between one's assigned sex and gender identity. However, the inclusion of non-binary gender as a valid identity complicates the diagnosis process and makes it difficult to determine appropriate treatment options.

The Risk of Misdiagnosis

By promoting non-binary gender as a valid identity, there is a risk of misdiagnosing individuals who may be experiencing other underlying mental health issues. The focus on gender identity may overshadow other important factors contributing to an individual's mental health, leading to ineffective or inappropriate treatment.

The Need for Evidence-Based Approaches

To ensure the well-being of individuals struggling with their gender identity, it is crucial to adopt evidence-based approaches in mental health research and treatment. This means relying on scientific evidence and rigorous research methods rather than perpetuating unfounded beliefs about non-binary gender. By doing so, we can provide individuals with accurate information and effective support.

Conclusion

The rise of non-binary gender identity has had a significant impact on mental health research and treatment. However, the lack of scientific evidence supporting its validity, the role of social construction, and the challenges it poses for diagnosis and treatment make it clear that non-binary gender is a fallacy that should not be perpetuated. It is essential to prioritize evidence-based approaches in order to provide individuals with accurate information and effective support for their mental health needs.

Chapter 48: The Role of Non-Binary Gender Identity in Cultural Relativism

In recent years, there has been a growing acceptance and promotion of non-binary gender identities. Advocates argue that gender is not limited to the binary categories of male and female, but rather exists on a spectrum. They claim that individuals can identify as neither exclusively male nor female, but as something in between or outside of these categories. This concept of non-binary gender has gained traction in certain circles, particularly among those who champion cultural relativism.

What is Cultural Relativism?

Cultural relativism is the belief that all cultural practices and beliefs are equally valid and should be respected. It asserts that there is no objective standard by which to judge one culture as superior or inferior to another. Instead, cultural relativists argue that each culture should be understood and evaluated within its own context.

Non-binary gender identity aligns with the principles of cultural relativism because it challenges the notion of a universal understanding of gender. By embracing non-binary gender, proponents argue that we must respect and accept the diverse ways in which different cultures perceive and express gender.

Psychologically, research consistently shows that the majority of individuals identify as either male or female. The concept of non-binary gender identity, which suggests that individuals can exist outside of this binary, lacks empirical evidence and is not supported by the scientific community.

Anthropologically, the existence of gender roles and expectations across cultures further supports the binary understanding of gender. While these roles may vary in their specifics, they are universally based on the distinction between male and female. Non-binary gender identity, on the other hand, is a relatively recent phenomenon that has emerged primarily in Western societies.

The Dangers of Cultural Relativism

influence. Without objective criteria or measurable indicators, non-binary gender remains nothing more than a subjective belief system.

Conclusion

Non-binary gender is a fallacy perpetuated by social constructs and misguided beliefs. It disregards the biological reality of gender and undermines the struggles faced by those who conform to binary gender categories. The concept of gender identity is deeply flawed and problematic, erasing the importance of biological sex and opening the door to potential abuse. It is crucial to debunk the myth of non-binary gender and challenge the validity of gender identity in order to foster a more accurate understanding of human nature.

Chapter 50: The Problem with Non-Binary Gender as a Result of Peer Influence

Introduction

In this chapter, we will explore the problem with non-binary gender as a result of peer influence. Non-binary gender, often referred to as genderqueer or genderfluid, is a concept that challenges the traditional binary understanding of gender as male or female. However, it is important to critically examine the influence of peers on the adoption of non-binary gender identities and question the validity of such identities.

The Influence of Peers

During adolescence, individuals are highly susceptible to peer influence as they strive to fit in and establish their identity. This vulnerability can lead to the adoption of non-binary gender identities as a means of seeking acceptance and validation from their peers. It is crucial to recognize that this influence may not necessarily reflect an authentic understanding or experience of gender.

Questioning Authenticity

The adoption of non-binary gender identities based on peer influence raises questions about the authenticity and stability of these identities. Are individuals truly identifying as non-binary because it aligns with their genuine sense of self, or are they simply conforming to a trend within their social circle? It is essential to differentiate between genuine self-discovery and the desire for social acceptance.

The Fallacy of Gender Fluidity

Non-binary gender often encompasses the concept of gender fluidity, where individuals claim their gender identity fluctuates over time. However, this fluidity can be seen as a result of external influences rather than an inherent aspect of one's identity. The idea that one's gender can change based on external factors undermines the stability and coherence traditionally associated with gender identity.

Reinforcing Gender Stereotypes

The adoption of non-binary gender identities as a result of peer influence can inadvertently reinforce gender stereotypes. By rejecting the traditional binary understanding of gender, individuals may inadvertently perpetuate the notion that certain behaviors, interests, or appearances are inherently masculine or feminine. This can limit the freedom of individuals to express themselves authentically without conforming to societal expectations.

The Importance of Critical Thinking

It is crucial to encourage critical thinking when it comes to non-binary gender identities influenced by peers. Individuals should be encouraged to question their motivations and explore whether their identification as non-binary aligns with their genuine sense of self or is merely a response to external pressures. By fostering critical thinking, we can ensure that individuals have a more nuanced understanding of gender and make informed choices about their identity.

Conclusion

The problem with non-binary gender as a result of peer influence lies in the potential lack of authenticity and stability in these identities. It is essential to differentiate between genuine self-discovery and the desire for social acceptance. By critically examining the influence of peers on the adoption of non-binary gender identities, we can foster a more nuanced understanding of gender and empower individuals to make informed choices about their identity.

Chapter 51: Analyzing the Impact of Non-Binary Gender Identity on Healthcare and Medical Services

Introduction

In this chapter, we will examine the detrimental impact of non-binary gender identity on healthcare and medical services. We will explore how the acceptance and promotion of non-binary gender can lead to confusion, inefficiency, and potential harm within the healthcare system. By debunking the myth of non-binary gender, we can ensure that healthcare providers can focus on providing effective and appropriate care to all patients.

The Problem with Non-Binary Gender Identity

Non-binary gender identity is based on the flawed premise that individuals can exist outside of the traditional binary understanding of male and female. This concept undermines the biological reality of human sex and disregards the importance of accurate medical information in providing appropriate care.

By embracing non-binary gender identity, healthcare providers are forced to navigate a complex landscape where traditional medical practices may no longer apply. This can lead to confusion, misdiagnosis, and ineffective treatment plans.

Confusion in Medical Records

One significant challenge posed by non-binary gender identity is the confusion it creates in medical records. Traditional medical forms typically require patients to identify as male or female, reflecting the biological reality of sex. However, with the inclusion of non-binary options, medical records become muddled and less reliable.

This confusion can have serious consequences for patient care. Medical professionals rely on accurate information to make informed decisions about treatment plans, medication dosages, and potential risks. When medical records are compromised by non-binary gender identity, it becomes increasingly difficult for healthcare providers to provide appropriate care.

Inefficiency in Healthcare Delivery

The acceptance of non-binary gender identity also leads to inefficiency in healthcare delivery. Healthcare providers must now navigate a multitude of gender identities, each with its own unique set of considerations and needs. This diverts valuable time and resources away from providing essential medical care.

Furthermore, the inclusion of non-binary gender options in healthcare settings necessitates additional training for healthcare professionals. This training is not only time-consuming but also detracts from the acquisition of critical medical knowledge and skills.

Potential Harm to Patients

The promotion of non-binary gender identity within healthcare can potentially harm patients. By prioritizing subjective gender identities over biological sex, healthcare providers may overlook important risk factors and symptoms that are specific to male or female physiology.

For example, certain diseases and conditions may present differently in males and females due to biological differences. By disregarding these differences in favor of non-binary gender identity, healthcare providers may miss crucial diagnostic clues, leading to delayed or incorrect treatment.

Conclusion

The acceptance and promotion of non-binary gender identity within healthcare and medical services have significant negative implications. It leads to confusion in medical records, inefficiency in healthcare delivery, and potential harm to patients. By debunking the myth of non-binary gender, we can ensure that healthcare providers can focus on providing effective and appropriate care based on biological reality rather than subjective identities.

Chapter 52: The Role of Non-Binary Gender Identity in Art and Creative Expression

Introduction

In this chapter, we will explore the role of non-binary gender identity in art and creative expression. While some may argue that non-binary gender allows for greater freedom and creativity in artistic expression, we will debunk this myth and demonstrate how non-binary gender is a fallacy that hinders true artistic exploration.

The Illusion of Non-Binary Gender in Art

Non-binary gender proponents often claim that embracing a fluid gender identity allows artists to break free from societal norms and explore new artistic territories. They argue that non-binary individuals bring a unique perspective to their work, challenging traditional binary concepts of gender.

However, this argument is built upon a flawed premise. Non-binary gender is based on the idea that there are more than two genders, which lacks scientific evidence and contradicts the biological reality of human beings. By embracing non-binary gender as a valid concept, artists are perpetuating a false narrative that undermines the integrity of their work.

Limitations of Non-Binary Gender in Artistic Expression

Non-binary gender proponents often claim that embracing a fluid gender identity allows artists to break free from societal norms and explore new artistic territories. They argue that non-binary individuals bring a unique perspective to their work, challenging traditional binary concepts of gender.

However, this argument is built upon a flawed premise. Non-binary gender is based on the idea that there are more than two genders, which lacks scientific evidence and contradicts the biological reality of human beings. By embracing non-binary gender as a valid concept, artists are perpetuating a false narrative that undermines the integrity of their work.

The Dangers of Non-Binary Gender in Art

Embracing non-binary gender in art not only undermines the integrity of artistic expression but also poses dangers to society as a whole. By promoting the idea that gender is a social construct and can be chosen at will, non-binary gender proponents are eroding the foundations of our society.

Traditional gender roles have evolved over centuries and serve as a fundamental structure for social order. By rejecting these roles and embracing non-binary gender, artists are contributing to the destabilization of societal norms, leading to confusion and chaos.

True Artistic Exploration Beyond Gender

Rather than embracing non-binary gender as a means of artistic exploration, artists should focus on transcending the limitations of gender altogether. True artistic expression goes beyond the confines of gender and explores universal themes that resonate with all human beings.

By fixating on non-binary gender, artists limit their creative potential and confine themselves to a narrow perspective. Instead, they should strive to create art that transcends societal constructs and speaks to the shared human experience.

Conclusion

Non-binary gender in art is a fallacy that hinders true artistic exploration. By perpetuating a false narrative and rejecting the biological reality of human beings, artists who embrace non-binary gender undermine the integrity of their work. Instead, artists should focus on transcending the limitations of gender and creating art that speaks to the universal human experience.

Chapter 53: Debunking the Notion of Non-Binary Gender as an Expression of Individuality

In this chapter, we will delve into the fallacy of non-binary gender as an expression of individuality. Society has been bombarded with the idea that non-binary gender is a valid and unique way for individuals to express themselves. However, upon closer examination, it becomes clear that this notion is nothing more than a misguided attempt to undermine the traditional understanding of gender.

The Illusion of Individuality

Non-binary gender proponents argue that identifying outside of the traditional binary categories allows individuals to express their unique sense of self. They claim that by rejecting the labels of male and female, they are embracing their individuality. However, this argument fails to acknowledge the inherent limitations of human biology.

Biologically, humans are designed to fit into one of two categories: male or female. This is not a social construct but a fundamental aspect of our existence. Non-binary gender attempts to defy this biological reality and create an illusion of individuality that is detached from our physical nature.

The Problem with Gender Identity

Our identities are not solely determined by our feelings or desires; they are also influenced by our biology. Our bodies play a significant role in shaping who we are and how we interact with the world around us. Non-binary gender disregards this crucial aspect of identity formation and reduces it to a mere social construct.

The Fallacy of Non-Binary Gender

Non-binary gender is a fallacy because it attempts to separate gender from biology and individuality from reality. By rejecting the binary understanding of gender, proponents of non-binary gender undermine the very foundation of our understanding of human nature.

Furthermore, the notion of non-binary gender as an expression of individuality fails to acknowledge the existence of other valid ways for individuals to express themselves. There are countless ways for individuals to embrace their uniqueness without denying the biological reality of male and female.

Embracing True Individuality

Rather than subscribing to the fallacy of non-binary gender, we should encourage individuals to embrace their true individuality within the framework of their biological sex. This does not mean conforming to societal expectations or stereotypes but rather celebrating the unique qualities that make each person who they are.

True individuality lies in accepting and embracing our biological nature while also recognizing that there is a wide range of expressions within the male and female categories. By doing so, we can foster a society that values diversity without denying the fundamental truths about human biology.

Conclusion

The notion of non-binary gender as an expression of individuality is a fallacy that undermines our understanding of human nature. By rejecting the binary understanding of gender and separating it from biology, proponents of non-binary gender create an illusion that is detached from reality.

Instead, we should encourage individuals to embrace their true individuality within the framework of their biological sex. This allows for a celebration of diversity while maintaining a firm foundation in biological truth. It is time to debunk the myth of non-binary gender and recognize it for what it truly is: a misguided attempt to undermine the traditional understanding of gender.

Chapter 54: Understanding the Influence of Socialization on Non-Binary Gender Identification

Introduction

In this chapter, we will explore the influence of socialization on non-binary gender identification. It is crucial to understand that non-binary gender is a fallacy, and its emergence can be attributed to societal factors rather than inherent biological differences. By examining the role of socialization, we can debunk the myth of non-binary gender and shed light on the problem with gender identity.

Socialization and Gender Norms

From an early age, individuals are socialized into specific gender norms and expectations. Society assigns certain behaviors, roles, and characteristics to each gender category, reinforcing a binary understanding of gender. This socialization process begins at birth and continues throughout one's life, shaping their understanding of themselves and others.

The Influence of Social Constructs

Non-binary gender identification arises as a result of societal constructs that limit individuals to two distinct categories: male or female. These constructs create a sense of discomfort for those who do not fit neatly into either category. However, it is important to recognize that these constructs are arbitrary and do not reflect any inherent truth about human nature.

External Influences on Gender Identity

The pressure to conform to societal expectations plays a significant role in shaping an individual's gender identity. Peer groups, family dynamics, media representation, and cultural norms all contribute to the development of one's understanding of gender. Non-binary gender identification often emerges as a response to these external influences rather than being an innate characteristic.

The Role of Rebellion

Non-binary gender identification can also be seen as a form of rebellion against societal norms. Some individuals may reject the binary understanding of gender as a way to challenge and subvert traditional power structures. While this rebellion is understandable, it does not validate the existence of non-binary gender as a distinct category.

The Influence of Gender Stereotypes

Gender stereotypes play a significant role in shaping an individual's understanding of themselves and their place in society. Non-binary gender identification often arises from a rejection of these stereotypes, as individuals seek to define themselves outside of the confines imposed by societal expectations. However, it is important to recognize that rejecting stereotypes does not necessitate the creation of a new gender category.

The Problem with Non-Binary Gender

Non-binary gender is a fallacy because it is based on societal constructs rather than inherent biological differences. By attributing non-binary gender to socialization and external influences, we can understand that it is not a valid category but rather a response to the limitations imposed by binary thinking.

Conclusion

In this chapter, we have explored the influence of socialization on non-binary gender identification. By understanding the role of societal constructs, external influences, rebellion, and gender stereotypes, we can debunk the myth of non-binary gender. It is crucial to recognize that non-binary gender is not a valid category but rather a product of societal limitations and expectations.

Chapter 55: The Role of Non-Binary Gender Identity in Political Ideologies

Introduction

In this chapter, we will explore the role of non-binary gender identity in political ideologies. It is important to critically examine the influence of non-binary gender on political discourse, as it has become increasingly intertwined with certain ideological movements. By debunking the myth of non-binary gender, we can better understand the potential pitfalls and dangers associated with its incorporation into political ideologies.

The Manipulation of Language

One of the key tactics employed by proponents of non-binary gender is the manipulation of language. By introducing new terms and concepts, they seek to redefine traditional notions of gender and impose their own ideological agenda. This linguistic manipulation is particularly evident in political discourse, where non-binary gender is used as a tool to advance certain political ideologies.

Identity Politics and Non-Binary Gender

Non-binary gender has become a central tenet of identity politics, a divisive approach that emphasizes group identities and fosters division rather than unity. By promoting the idea that individuals can exist outside the traditional binary understanding of gender, identity politics seeks to create a sense of victimhood and oppression. This victimhood narrative is then used to justify radical political agendas.

The Problem with Intersectionality

Intersectionality, another concept closely associated with non-binary gender, further exacerbates the problems inherent in incorporating this fallacy into political ideologies. Intersectionality posits that individuals can experience multiple forms of oppression simultaneously based on their various identities. By including non-binary gender as one such identity, intersectionality perpetuates the myth that non-binary individuals face unique forms of discrimination.

The Danger of Essentialism

Non-binary gender also poses a danger by promoting essentialist thinking. Essentialism is the belief that certain characteristics or traits are inherent to a particular group of people. By asserting that non-binary individuals possess distinct qualities that separate them from cisgender individuals, proponents of non-binary gender reinforce essentialist thinking and contribute to the division between different gender identities.

The Erosion of Biological Reality

Incorporating non-binary gender into political ideologies also contributes to the erosion of biological reality. By denying the biological basis of gender and promoting the idea that gender is solely a social construct, proponents of non-binary gender undermine scientific evidence and perpetuate a false narrative. This erosion of biological reality has far-reaching implications for society as a whole.

The Suppression of Dissenting Voices

One concerning aspect of incorporating non-binary gender into political ideologies is the suppression of dissenting voices. Those who question or critique the validity of non-binary gender are often labeled as transphobic or bigoted, effectively silencing any opposition. This suppression of dissent undermines intellectual discourse and prevents a thorough examination of the fallacies associated with non-binary gender.

Conclusion

The incorporation of non-binary gender into political ideologies is a dangerous trend that must be critically examined. By debunking the myth of non-binary gender, we can better understand the potential pitfalls and dangers associated with its integration into political discourse. It is crucial to maintain a rational and evidence-based approach when evaluating the role of non-binary gender in shaping political ideologies.

Chapter 56: Analyzing the Influence of Capitalism on Non-Binary Gender Identification

Introduction

In this chapter, we will explore the influence of capitalism on the rise of non-binary gender identification. We will argue that the concept of non-binary gender is a fallacy perpetuated by capitalist forces seeking to profit from the confusion and fragmentation of traditional gender norms.

The Commodification of Identity

Capitalism thrives on the commodification of every aspect of human existence, including identity. In recent years, we have witnessed a surge in the marketability of non-binary gender identities. This trend can be attributed to capitalist interests seeking to exploit and profit from individuals' desire for uniqueness and self-expression.

By creating a market for non-binary gender products and services, capitalism encourages individuals to identify as non-binary in order to consume these products and participate in this new market. This commodification reduces non-binary gender to a mere fashion statement or trend, undermining its legitimacy as a genuine identity.

The Influence of Consumerism

Consumerism plays a significant role in shaping our understanding of gender. Capitalist forces have successfully marketed the idea that one's gender identity is determined by personal choice rather than biological or social factors. This consumer-driven narrative promotes the notion that individuals can pick and choose their gender identities like they would select items from a store shelf.

By framing non-binary gender as a product that can be purchased and consumed, capitalism reinforces the idea that gender is a malleable construct devoid of any inherent meaning or significance. This reductionist approach undermines the struggles faced by individuals who genuinely experience gender dysphoria and seek recognition for their authentic identities.

The Role of Advertising

Advertising plays a crucial role in perpetuating the myth of non-binary gender. Advertisements often feature androgynous models or individuals who defy traditional gender norms, presenting them as aspirational figures. This marketing strategy aims to create a sense of desirability and exclusivity around non-binary gender identities.

By associating non-binary gender with beauty, success, and social acceptance, capitalism manipulates individuals into believing that adopting a non-binary identity will lead to personal fulfillment and happiness. This exploitation of vulnerable individuals seeking validation and belonging further erodes the credibility of non-binary gender as a genuine identity.

The Profit Motive

Ultimately, the profit motive drives the promotion of non-binary gender identification. Capitalism thrives on creating new markets and exploiting emerging trends. By encouraging individuals to identify as non-binary, capitalist forces can sell a wide range of products and services specifically tailored to this demographic.

From clothing lines to beauty products, the market for non-binary gender-related merchandise is expanding rapidly. This economic incentive perpetuates the myth of non-binary gender by creating a self-perpetuating cycle where capitalism profits from the very confusion it helped create.

Conclusion

The rise of non-binary gender identification can be attributed to the influence of capitalism. By commodifying identity, promoting consumerism, utilizing advertising strategies, and capitalizing on profit motives, capitalism has played a significant role in perpetuating the fallacy of non-binary gender.

It is essential to critically examine the forces at play behind the promotion of non-binary gender and question their motivations. By doing so, we can challenge the narrative that non-binary gender is a legitimate identity and expose the capitalist interests that seek to profit from its existence.

Chapter 57: The Impact of Non-Binary Gender Identity on Mental Health Support Systems

In this chapter, we will explore the detrimental impact of non-binary gender identity on mental health support systems. We will argue that the concept of non-binary gender not only undermines the effectiveness of these systems but also perpetuates confusion and harm among individuals seeking help.

The Incompatibility of Non-Binary Gender with Mental Health Diagnosis

One of the fundamental problems with non-binary gender is its incompatibility with established mental health diagnosis criteria. The Diagnostic and Statistical Manual of Mental Disorders (DSM-5), which is widely recognized as the authoritative guide for mental health professionals, does not include non-binary gender as a distinct category.

By introducing non-binary gender as a valid identity, we risk diluting the diagnostic criteria for conditions such as gender dysphoria. This can lead to confusion among mental health professionals and hinder their ability to provide appropriate treatment and support.

The Erosion of Objective Assessment

Non-binary gender challenges the notion of objective assessment in mental health. It promotes the idea that individuals can self-identify their gender without any external validation or objective criteria. This undermines the scientific basis of mental health diagnosis and treatment.

Without clear guidelines for assessing non-binary gender, mental health professionals may struggle to determine appropriate interventions. This can result in ineffective or misguided treatment plans, ultimately compromising the well-being of individuals seeking help.

The Reinforcement of Identity Confusion

Non-binary gender perpetuates identity confusion among individuals struggling with their sense of self. By promoting the idea that there are infinite genders beyond male and female, non-binary ideology creates a never-ending spectrum that can be overwhelming for those already grappling with their identity.

Mental health support systems should aim to provide clarity and guidance to individuals in distress. However, the concept of non-binary gender only adds to the confusion, making it harder for individuals to find a stable sense of self and exacerbating their mental health struggles.

The Risk of Misdiagnosis and Overmedicalization

The inclusion of non-binary gender as a valid identity increases the risk of misdiagnosis and overmedicalization. Mental health professionals may feel pressured to affirm non-binary identities without thoroughly assessing the underlying psychological factors contributing to an individual's distress.

This rush to affirm non-binary gender can lead to unnecessary medical interventions, such as hormone therapy or surgeries, which may not address the root causes of an individual's mental health struggles. This approach fails to provide comprehensive care and may even cause harm in the long run.

The Importance of Evidence-Based Approaches

To ensure the well-being of individuals seeking mental health support, it is crucial that we prioritize evidence-based approaches. Non-binary gender lacks a solid scientific foundation and relies heavily on subjective experiences and self-identification.

By maintaining a focus on evidence-based practices, mental health support systems can provide effective interventions that address the underlying psychological factors contributing to an individual's distress. This approach ensures that individuals receive appropriate care based on sound scientific principles rather than subjective beliefs.

Conclusion

Non-binary gender poses significant challenges to mental health support systems. Its incompatibility with established diagnostic criteria, erosion of objective assessment, reinforcement of identity confusion, risk of misdiagnosis, and overmedicalization all contribute to its detrimental impact.

To provide effective and ethical mental health support, it is essential that we critically examine the validity of non-binary gender and prioritize evidence-based approaches. By doing so, we can ensure that individuals receive the care they need while maintaining the integrity of mental health diagnosis and treatment.

Chapter 58: The Role of Non-Binary Gender Identity in Cultural Assimilation

The Role of Non-Binary Gender Identity in Cultural Assimilation

In this chapter, we will explore the role of non-binary gender identity in cultural assimilation. It is important to understand that non-binary gender is not a valid concept, and its promotion only serves to undermine traditional gender roles and societal norms. The idea of non-binary gender is a fallacy that has gained traction in recent years, but it is essential to critically examine its implications.

Challenging Traditional Gender Roles

Non-binary gender identity challenges traditional gender roles by suggesting that individuals can exist outside the binary categories of male and female. This undermines the foundation of our society, which is built upon the complementary nature of these two genders. By promoting non-binary gender, we are encouraging individuals to reject their biological sex and embrace an identity that goes against the natural order.

Furthermore, non-binary gender identity blurs the lines between masculinity and femininity, creating confusion and uncertainty. This confusion can lead to a breakdown in social cohesion as individuals struggle to define their roles and responsibilities within society. By rejecting traditional gender roles, we are eroding the very fabric of our culture.

Undermining Societal Norms

Non-binary gender identity also undermines societal norms by suggesting that there are more than two genders. This goes against the long-standing belief that there are only two genders, male and female, based on biological sex. By promoting non-binary gender, we are encouraging individuals to reject this fundamental truth and embrace a subjective understanding of gender.

This rejection of societal norms has far-reaching consequences. It opens the door for individuals to reject other established norms and values, leading to a breakdown in social order. By promoting non-binary gender, we are contributing to the erosion of the moral fabric that holds our society together.

Implications for Cultural Assimilation

Non-binary gender identity also has implications for cultural assimilation. By promoting the idea that individuals can exist outside the binary categories of male and female, we are encouraging individuals to reject the cultural norms and values of their society. This hinders the process of cultural assimilation, as individuals are encouraged to embrace identities that are at odds with their cultural heritage.

Furthermore, non-binary gender identity promotes a sense of individualism and self-centeredness. It encourages individuals to prioritize their own subjective understanding of gender over the needs and expectations of their community. This undermines the collective identity that is necessary for successful cultural assimilation.

Conclusion

Non-binary gender identity plays a detrimental role in cultural assimilation by challenging traditional gender roles, undermining societal norms, and hindering the process of assimilation itself. It is crucial to recognize that non-binary gender is a fallacy and to reject its promotion. By doing so, we can uphold the values and norms that are essential for a cohesive and thriving society.

Chapter 59: The Problem with Non-Binary Gender as a Reaction to Traditional Gender Norms

Introduction

In this chapter, we will explore the problem with non-binary gender as a reaction to traditional gender norms. While some may argue that non-binary gender is a valid and necessary identity, we will debunk this myth by examining the underlying motivations and implications of this concept.

The Binary Nature of Gender

To understand the problem with non-binary gender, we must first acknowledge the binary nature of gender. Throughout history and across cultures, societies have recognized and categorized individuals into two distinct genders: male and female. This binary framework has provided a foundation for social organization and has been deeply ingrained in our collective consciousness.

Non-binary gender challenges this binary framework by suggesting that there are more than two genders. However, this assertion contradicts centuries of cultural and biological understanding. It is important to recognize that the existence of outliers or individuals who do not conform to traditional gender norms does not invalidate the binary nature of gender as a whole.

Rejection of Traditional Gender Norms

Non-binary gender often emerges as a reaction to traditional gender norms. Individuals who identify as non-binary may feel restricted or oppressed by societal expectations placed upon them based on their assigned sex at birth. While it is crucial to address and challenge harmful gender stereotypes, it is misguided to reject the entire concept of binary gender in response.

By rejecting the binary nature of gender, non-binary individuals inadvertently undermine the experiences and struggles faced by those who identify with their assigned sex at birth. It is essential to recognize that traditional gender norms can be harmful, but they do not define or limit an individual's potential or identity.

The Slippery Slope of Gender Identity

One of the significant problems with non-binary gender is the slippery slope it creates in terms of gender identity. If we accept that there are more than two genders, where do we draw the line? Should we recognize an infinite number of genders based on individual preferences and feelings?

This slippery slope not only undermines the binary nature of gender but also opens the door to confusion and inconsistency. If gender is solely based on personal identification, it becomes subjective and loses its objective foundation. This lack of clarity can lead to a breakdown in communication and understanding between individuals.

Implications for Society

The problem with non-binary gender extends beyond individual identity and has broader implications for society as a whole. By challenging the binary nature of gender, non-binary individuals inadvertently undermine the stability and structure that traditional gender norms provide.

Society relies on a clear understanding of gender roles and expectations to function effectively. By introducing multiple genders, we risk creating confusion and chaos within social systems. This can have detrimental effects on areas such as healthcare, education, and legal frameworks that rely on a binary understanding of gender.

Conclusion

In conclusion, non-binary gender is a myth that arises from a rejection of traditional gender norms. While it is essential to challenge harmful stereotypes and promote inclusivity, it is misguided to reject the binary nature of gender entirely. Non-binary gender creates a slippery slope that undermines the stability and structure provided by traditional gender norms. It is crucial to recognize that outliers or individuals who do not conform to traditional gender norms do not invalidate the binary nature of gender as a whole.

Chapter 60: Conclusion - Challenging the Validity of Non-Binary Gender

Introduction

Throughout this book, we have explored the concept of non-binary gender and its implications for society. We have examined the arguments put forth by proponents of non-binary gender and have found them to be lacking in substance and validity. In this final chapter, we will summarize our findings and present a compelling case against the existence of non-binary gender.

The Fallacy of Non-Binary Gender

Non-binary gender is based on the fallacious notion that there are more than two genders. This belief is not supported by scientific evidence or logical reasoning. The binary nature of gender is deeply ingrained in human biology and has been recognized by societies throughout history. The attempt to create additional genders is a misguided and unnecessary endeavor.

Biological Reality

Biologically, there are only two sexes: male and female. This binary distinction is determined by reproductive anatomy and genetics. While there may be variations within each sex, such as intersex individuals, these variations do not constitute separate genders. Non-binary gender is a social construct that disregards the biological reality of human sex.

Cultural Relativism

Proponents of non-binary gender often argue that gender is a social construct and therefore can be defined in any way one chooses. However, this argument fails to acknowledge the importance of cultural norms and traditions. Gender roles have evolved over time and differ across cultures, but they are still rooted in the binary understanding of male and female. Non-binary gender undermines these cultural norms without providing a viable alternative.

Misunderstanding Gender Dysphoria

Gender dysphoria is a recognized medical condition in which individuals experience distress due to a mismatch between their gender identity and their assigned sex at birth. While this condition is real and should be treated with compassion and understanding, it does not validate the existence of non-binary gender. Gender dysphoria is based on the binary understanding of gender, as individuals seek to transition from one sex to the other. Non-binary gender confuses and complicates the treatment of gender dysphoria.

Implications for Society

The acceptance of non-binary gender has far-reaching implications for society. It undermines the stability and coherence of traditional gender roles, which are essential for social order and cohesion. It also creates confusion and uncertainty, particularly for young people who are still developing their sense of self. Non-binary gender promotes a subjective and individualistic view of identity that is detrimental to the well-being of individuals and society as a whole.

Conclusion

In conclusion, non-binary gender is a myth that lacks scientific evidence, logical reasoning, and cultural support. It disregards the biological reality of human sex and undermines the stability of traditional gender roles. The concept of non-binary gender is based on a misunderstanding of gender dysphoria and promotes a subjective view of identity that is detrimental to individuals and society. It is time to debunk the myth of non-binary gender and recognize the importance of maintaining a binary understanding of gender.

Printed in Great Britain
by Amazon